+ create   design   *inspire*

{working

a showcase of graphic design alumni from montana state university

by Jeffrey Conger + Anne Garner + Ben Meyer + Stephanie Newman

Montana State University
School of Art

Working: A Showcase of Graphic Design Alumni from Montana State University
by Jeffrey Conger + Anne Garner + Ben Meyer + Stephanie Newman

Published by
Montana State University
School of Art
213 Haynes Hall
Bozeman, MT 59717
www.montana.edu/art

Printed by Pragati Printing USA Inc.
10 9 8 7 6 5 4 3 2 1

Book Editor: Jeffrey Conger
Project Coordinators: Anne Garner + Ben Meyer + Stephanie Newman
Production Coordinators: Bruce Barnhart + Patrick Jeske
Production Assistants: Jeanne Wagner + Mandi McCarthy-Rogers
Cover Design: Bryan Hintz
Photography: Ryan Wilson

ISBN 0-9766118-0-5

{ *table of contents*

Barry Ament	Ames Bros.	16-19
Jack Anderson	Hornall Anderson Design Works	20-23
Jennifer Bartlett	Tim Girvin	24-25
Kelly Bellcour	Wise Acre Studios	26-27
Benjamin Bennett	Massive Studios	28-29
Gregg Berryman	California State University	30-31
Dan Bilyeu	International Game Technology	32-33
Tim Braun	Fossil Creative	34-35
Bill Brown	Freelance Illustrator	36-37
Spencer Buck	K2 Sports	38-39
Jen Cox	Classic Ink	40-41
Jody Neil Creasman	Oregon College of Arts and Crafts	42-43
Mandy Cufley	Lucky Girl Designs	44-45
William Cullen	Freelance Designer	46-47
Nat Cundy	Custom Kingpin	48-49
Nick Daniels	Great Falls Tribune	50-51
Craig Davidson	Civic Design	52-53
Korey Doll	Edwards Design	54-55
Kristen Drumheller	Montana State University	56-57
Scott Edmonds	Nomura	58-59
Mary Edwards	Murdoch's	60-61
Robyn Egloff	Mercury Advertising	62-63
Matthew Grimes	Info Space	64-65
Blaine Halvorson	Junk Food Inc.	66-69
Adam Karig Haynes	Adidas	70-71
Dave Hebert	Evergreen Aviation	72-73
Carl Heidle	Quisenberry Marketing	74-75
Eric Heidle	Wendt Advertising	76-77
Hiller Higman	Bootleg Enterprise	78-79
Josh Huisenga	Chalkbox Studio	80-81
Danielle Hurd	Studio 1212	82-83
Patrick Jeske	Co-operate Design Co.	84-85
Jason Johnson	Freelance Designer	86-87
Russ Kaiser	Freelance Illustrator	88-89
Kris Krieg	Vivify	90-91
Barbara Kuhr	Plunkett+Kuhr	92-93
Mary Kysar	Makelike Design	94-95
Rebekah Lane	Nintendo of America	96
Jill Anderson-Story	V-Design Inc.	97
Heidi Lauman	Freelance Designer/Illustrator	98-99
Nichole Lear	45 Degrees North	100-101
Dana Lytle	Planet Propaganda	102-105
Angie Mangels	Earthtalk Studios	106-107
Matt Meeks	Moo Interactive Inc.	108-109
Raelene Mercer	Sublime Miami	110-111
Robert Mercer	Starbucks Coffee	112-113
Molly A. Merica	Merica Design	114-115
Jenae Neeson	Clark Creative Group	116-117
Erik "Ole" Nelson	Media Station Design Works	118-119
Kietra Nelson	Classic Ink	120-121
Kurt J. Palmquist	Ripple Marketing	122-123
Carol Patterson	Life-Link International	124-125
Julie Pfleger	Wild West Shirt Company	126-127
Catherine Pilgrim	Modern Luxury Magazines	128-129
Bridget Preston	Washington Athletic Club	130-131
Heather M. Preston	Scott Publishing Inc.	132-133
Carlos Radillo	Wild West Shirt Works	134-135
Robert Rath	Freelance Illustrator	136-137
Annie Regnier	Columbia Sportswear	138-139
Sue Savage	Coldwater Creek	140-141
Karen Schmidt	K-Graphics	142-143
Christian Schultz	Northwave/Piva Co.	144-145
Coby Schultz	Ames Bros.	146-149
Jennifer Simon-Becker	Big Sky Carvers	150-151
Richard A. Smith	Double Entendre Inc.	152-153
Daniel P. Smith	Double Entendre Inc.	152-153
Drake Socie	Walcott-Ayers Group	154-155
Amy Sowers	Wantulok Design	156-157
Ryan Tillett	Future Farm	158-159
Cheyenne Troupe	Cheyenne Rivers Studio	160-161
Ixtla Vaughan	IDesign	162-163
Matt Wellman	Nike	164-165
Jamie Willett-Hurd	Mercury Advertising	166-167
Jeff Williams	Tower Records	168-169
Marla Wyche	Mad Magazine	170-171

RICHARD HELZER
director, school of art

{ *acknowledgments*

For the School of Art to be involved in publishing a book of this magnitude is very exciting and it is important that plaudits be given to those who have worked so hard on this project. There are many people who have contributed to the success of *Working*. Special thanks go to the graphic design professors Jeffrey Conger, Anne Garner, Ben Meyer and Stephanie Newman, and the current adjunct design faculty Bruce Barnhart and Patrick Jeske. Over the years, many additional adjunct faculty have left their mark on our design program. Most recently they include Ben Bennett, Rachel Hundhausen, Robyn Egloff, Kris Ellingsen, Daphne Gillam, Kurt Palmquist, Rob Rath and Karen Schmidt.

Thanks also go to the Montana State University Foundation Director David Gibson and Vice President for Research and Creativity Tom McCoy for funding assistance, and to all of the extraordinary, talented alumni featured in this book. A special thank you goes to all 32 seniors in the 2005 graphic design class listed on page 175, and to Bryan Hintz the talented senior from Wolf Point who created the cover artwork. It is also important to note that this book would not have happened without the persistence and vision of Associate Professor Jeffrey Conger. We are extremely proud of *Working* and its demonstration of the great successes of the Graphic Design program in the School of Art at Montana State University.

JEFFREY CONGER
associate professor of graphic design

{ introduction

The design studio is a place to get work done. It is an environment that transforms creativity into commerce. Every magazine you have touched was made by a designer. Every package ever purchased was laid out by a commercial artist. Graphic design is the profession that delivers artwork to the business world; it utilizes the creative skills of a fine artist combined with the marketing sense of a successful entrepreneur. The act of creating design is tangible. You see it daily, you hold it in your hands, it teaches, informs and entertains. With 75 alumni featured in this book, I am sure there are designs you will recognize. Being a professional means that your artwork is in the public eye. Flipping through the pages you will notice several designers' work that has gained national attention including Coby Schultz and Barry Ament of Ames Bros. whose posters for Pearl Jam were recently published in the best selling hardcover book *Art of Modern Rock*. Several graphic designers with the entrepreneurial gene have forged their own companies often employing dozens. Jack Anderson of the notable Hornall Anderson Design Works rebranded the Seattle Sonics NBA basketball team as well at the iconic Space Needle. Blaine Halvorson, co-owner of Junk Food Inc. is the largest licensing t-shirt manufacturer in the world producing one million shirts per week. Dana Lytle, a founding partner of Planet Propaganda services an elite client list including Gary Fisher Bikes and JanSport, while Barbara Kuhr and her husband helped launch the visionary *Wired Magazine* over a decade ago. Being an educator a few of my favorite projects include the books written and designed by Gregg Berryman that are used as textbooks by hundreds of design programs across the country. Other successful alumni work in-house creating the artwork for major corporations. A few shown here are Rob Mercer at Starbucks, Matt Wellman at Nike, Rebekah Lane at Nintendo, Spencer Buck at K2 Sports, Jeff Williams at Tower Records, Annie Regnier at Columbia Sportswear, Adam Haynes at Adidas and Marla Wyche at *Mad Magazine*. Other designers like Robert Rath and Bill Brown have chosen the freelance illustrator life serving as hired guns for the creative world. Art is commerce. Look around and put a price on everything you can see. A culture without graphics, symbols or illustration is unimaginable.

ANNE GARNER
professor of graphic design

We consider it an asset to be part of a university. A university demands an education in a broad range of subjects from the sciences to the humanities. It also offers a variety of resources and experts. Graphic design is a field where the more general knowledge a designer possesses, the more intelligent are their solutions. In addition, as part of the School of Art, our students must take a substantial portion of studio classes in several of the fine arts mediums as well as five classes in art history. We are located in Montana which means being geographically isolated, separated from large cities with their flourishing design communities and their internship opportunities. Being in Montana also means cultural isolation for the large proportion of our students who grew up here. Yet, with the state's frontier past still in recent memory, we can expect that many students will possess Montana's frontier attributes of the well-developed work ethic and a sense of responsibility. Most students have jobs while in school; it is not uncommon for some to have a thirty to forty hour work week in addition to a full academic load. Most graduate with loans to pay off, so it didn't make sense to develop a design education with a narrow elitist focus. When the University's art program had been established a century earlier, its stated intent was to prepare the students for a commercial profession. We believe this is still a worthy goal. We don't want to turn out prima donnas. We want to prepare hardworking, creative, and responsible workers who will be valuable assets to future employers and clients. The value of our students' education is realized when they enter their chosen field of graphic design. The value is realized when they are working.

Graphic Design has become a popular major. In the 1980s the number of graphic design majors began to grow so quickly that accommodating them with our limited resources became a daunting task. Beyond the practical issues of limiting enrollment, the entire design faculty felt that having an oversized program would damage its effectiveness. We want to know who our students are. We want them to develop a sense of their own design style. Then we encourage them to develop that style as seriously as possible. We don't believe that there is only one correct way to design. It is important to us to have our students graduate with their personal vision intact. In order to limit enrollment we established a portfolio review ten years ago. Currently we screen out over half of the first year students prior to the intermediate level. *Working* is an effort to capture a cross-section of what some of our many students have achieved as professional graphic designers. It is a great satisfaction to their teachers to discover the broad variety of American businesses and culture that our Montana students are serving. They have come quite a distance from those first weeks in Introduction to Graphic Design class when they were nervous and confused, taking the first steps towards becoming graphic designers, dreaming that they would one day be . . . working.

STEPHANIE NEWMAN
professor of graphic design

At first glance Montana is not a place one expects to find a hotbed of design excellence. The alumni careers highlighted in this book testify that we must be doing something right. An amazing synergy exists in the graphic design area, a rare and possibly unique phenomenon in the academic world. The talents, skills, backgrounds, interests, and personalities of the four full-time faculty are complementary, while all share a common passion for design and teaching. The students are bright, talented, energetic, and diligent. It's a mix that works.

Now all students who pass portfolio review are required to purchase a laptop computer. This has had a profound effect on classroom dynamics and students' responsibility for their own equipment. As we hoped, students' grasp of computer skills has improved exponentially; we are able to spend more time on design and less on computer problems. Still, ours is a small program in a small town. While we cover a broad range of topics in our curriculum, we have chosen to emphasize problem solving, conceptualization, presentation, and individuality.

Our growing internship program allows an increasing number of juniors and seniors to get practical experience while they are still in school. Others get that experience on campus working for SUB Graphics, or designing for KGLT radio or ASMSU. Our newly instituted annual field trip grew out of a round table class discussion. For the past three falls, the seniors and four instructors have ridden a chartered bus to Seattle or Portland, spending three days visiting design firms, ad agencies, and new media companies, while also exploring the city, eating sushi and pad thai, meeting and visiting many of the alumni working in the area. Plans are underway for next year's return trip to Portland while other urban areas within driving distance are slated for future years.

The trip exposes students to professional practices, generates tremendous enthusiasm and pride in design as a profession, and melds the two sections of the class into one effective, supportive working group. In 1998 we introduced a final thesis for seniors, a capstone of their university experience. Students initiate their own projects. We urge them to combine other passions with design. The senior year and thesis semester in particular serve as a bridge from school to the working world. We want them to graduate with portfolios that will get jobs, able to present and promote themselves, independent, self-motivated, and confident. We take pride in having no house style, that our students graduate with their individuality intact. Our aim is for our graduates not only to be successful but also fulfilled as professional designers.

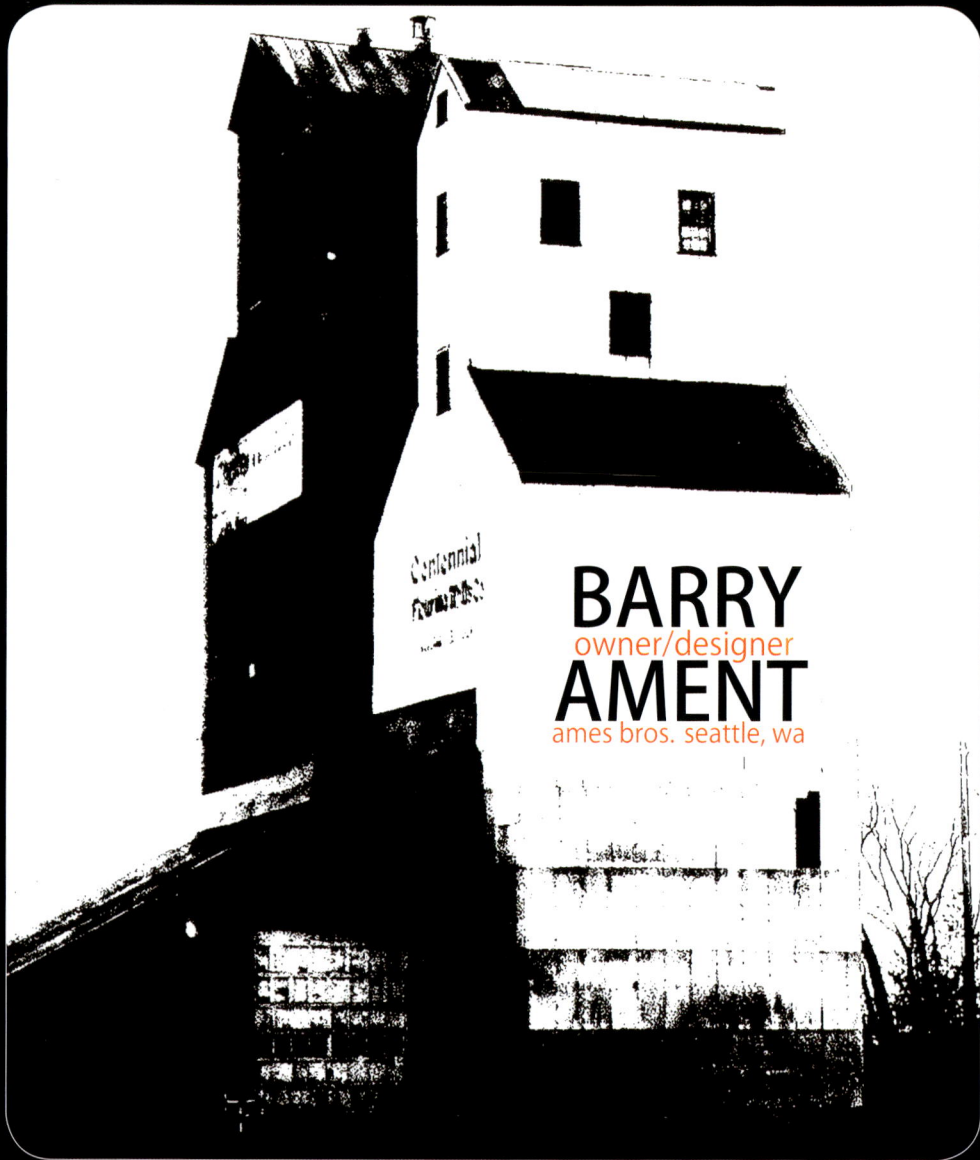

BARRY
owner/designer
AMENT
ames bros. seattle, wa

What advice would you give to a new graduate seeking employment?
First and foremost come with a strong portfolio and a basic understanding of the business at which you are interviewing. We get a lot of first in the phonebook drop-by's who are shown the door pretty quickly. If you aren't interested, why should I be? Also, don't act like you know it all, because you don't. Confidence is OK as long as there's a little bit of humility thrown in. **Where did you grow up?** Big Sandy, Montana. **How do you prefer your steak?** Medium Rare. **What is your favorite color?** Light Pink. **Any previous design employers?** No.

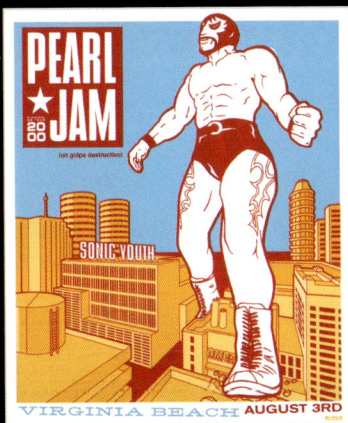

AMES BROS

POP. 02

barry ament

more AMES BROS

Known for their traditional silkscreen posters and design in the music and snowboard industries, AMES BROS continues to redefine the look of the northwest.

JACK ANDERSON
Founding Partner/Creative Director
Hornall Anderson Design Works
Seattle, WA

Hornall Anderson is an idea company committed to exceeding our client's goals and objectives. In order to develop breakthrough solutions, we apply a process and methodology that assures clear communication and consistent quality of our work

Q: What brought you to Seattle?

A: When I graduated from Montana State University in 1975, advertising was the only thing Montana offered in the design field. I knew I wanted to be in the West, so I was looking into either Denver or Seattle. Since I had an uncle working as an architect in Seattle, I connected with him and used my architectural background to begin my first job working in an architectural firm creating environmental design. At that time, Seattle represented something huge, exciting, influential and full of opportunity. Not to say it's not still all of those things, it just feels more like a town to me now.

Q: How was Hornall Anderson Design Works launched?

A: John Hornall and I first met when I was interviewing with design firms during my junior year of college. We stayed in contact for five and a half years before I was hired on to work with him in a design group at Cole & Weber for a year and a half. In 1982, John and I had the opportunity to form a partnership, which was the beginning of Hornall Anderson Design Works. The firm began designing literature systems for Princess Tours, and the business just grew from there.

sky City

SKYLINE

S·P·A·C·E

JACK ANDERSON Continued

Q: What are the essential steps to success?
A: Curiosity makes a person interesting. It's important to have a pulse on global culture and be informed about a lot of things. Project diversity, although not an essential step, can play a big part in a designer's success. Work ethic, not necessarily just IQ, will also yield success. Hard work and street smarts are very important in achieving this. Try to see things from different angles, and apply yourself to tasks involving other types of skills and solutions beyond your usual formula.

Q: What are your design influences or inspirations?
A: There is no "one" individual I admire more than another. My inspiration comes from a variety of sources: my staff, colleagues and contemporaries. I also find great inspiration in things outside the

o deck
tickets
520' viewing

skyline
check-in
100' events

sky city
check-in
360° dining

discipline, like architecture, industrial design, urban spaces, buildings and materials.

Q: Do you find yourself designing less and managing more?
A: Yes, I have responsibilities inherent to a management position. I take great pride and confidence in the team built around me. It is always my goal to get more engaged with clients and designers. I consider a 70-75% designer/client involvement a total success.

Q: What is your advice to upcoming designers?
A: Be confident, but exercise humility. Find a niche that fits your interests, get a foot in the door, be passionate and maintain a good work ethic. Having an interest in, and a love of, life and people will help you embrace diversity. That respect for diversity keeps things fresh, and dissuades you from falling into a set pattern regarding how you go about solving problems.

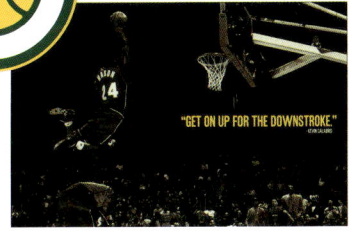

RENEW
RESPECT

"GET ON UP FOR THE DOWNSTROKE."

NEW GUY

GOAL IS TO BRING SON
CHAMPIONSHIP BACK
RE NEW

Sprint PCS

Jennifer Bartlett
Creative Director

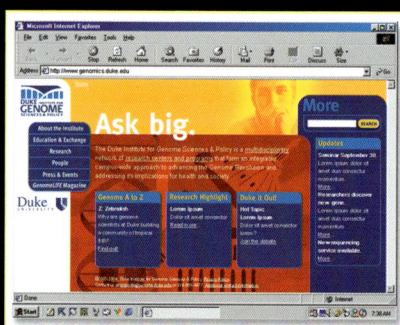

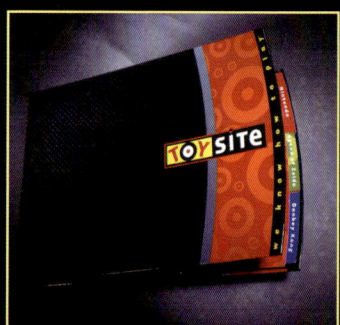

RVIN

Which area of design do you like most?

I like working on complete projects. I like establishing the brand positioning and personality, then visually exploring what the new brand should look like. I enjoy building all the design pieces from a firmly established foundation. I think the best projects are those with lots of collaboration.

What area in the arts would you like to improve?

There are many areas that I personally can improve on, but I am a generalist when it comes to art. I love to try new mediums and techniques. Because of my desire to try new things, I never get very good at any particular form of art, but I do have a great time in the process.

Who did you work for previously?

I worked for Vickerman Zachary Miller, an Engineering and Architecture firm in Oakland, California. I worked there for 10 years, ultimately leading the graphic design group before moving to Seattle. I freelanced in Seattle for a few months before being hired at Girvin as an Associate Designer.

Who inspires or drives you most?

There isn't one person or thing that inspires me. Anything I see throughout the day can inspire me in one way or another. It could be a shade of red on a billboard, or the way a building is reflected in a puddle. I love what I do, and the passion I have for my profession drives me to constantly strive to improve my work.

KELLY BELLCOUR
Wise Acre Studios
Bozeman, MT

What influences inspire you?
Old western, old school, learning something
new, fuzzy animals and anything that is funny!

" I've learned something
about design and myself
with every employment
opportunity. Real working
experience after school,
no matter how simple
is critical for getting a
sense of who you are
as a designer ".

Do you ever have time to sleep?
Sleep is a requirement for me to be productive
the following day. I find myself thinking projects
through more before I sit down and begin actual
work. Surprises and discoveries sometimes
happen, and when they do it's nice.

KELLY
BELLCOUR

Is working for yourself better than working for someone else?

For me, yes! I find it exciting to have a hand in how a business develops and to be able to shape its personality. Self-employment requires more discipline and giddy-up than simply being an employee. You become responsible for the work itself, and all other aspects associated with operating a company: finding insurance, hiring an accountant, taking out the trash. As your business grows, you may find yourself doing more administrative tasks and less design. It is often difficult to find true down time because you're more personally invested and always looking ahead to the next problem. Normal frustrations aside, being a self-employed designer has allowed my husband and me to live in Montana and support a family. . . and that's pretty darn good!

GOURMET
Pepper Blend

GOURMET
Lemon Pepper

GOURMET
All-Purpose Spice

"Lite"

Alpine Touch
NET WT. 4 OZ.

Alpine Touch
NET WT. 4 OZ.

Alpine Touch
NET WT. 4 OZ.

Through the Woods

EXPLORING NEW PATHS FOR CHILDREN
VOLUME II

FISHING MUSIC

FISHING MUSIC
A spirited mix of songs and tunes inspired by fish, fishing and rivers, performed by some of the country's finest acoustic musicians.

FISHING MUSIC
a collection of acoustic folk, blues & swing

FLY FISHING IN THE ROCKY MOUNTAINS *is more than a sum of its parts, and Ruby Springs Lodge is uniquely able to deliver the best of every element.*

Located on a stunning 700 acre ranch outside of Alder, Montana, Ruby Springs offers what has been described as the finest fly-fishing lodge experience in the country.

Ruby Springs Lodge is a powerful blend of exceptional outdoor experiences and impressive indoor amenities.

COME JOIN US
IN MONTANA

How does living and working in Bozeman affect your design?

Getting out of the office and doing something in nature factors into how we design by being able to relate to outdoor oriented industries as well as their prospective markets. How do you design for a backpacking company if you've never backpacked or never stuffed a pack before (and realized both can sometimes be pleasurable or painful)? A designer runs the risk of not identifying with the target market if they are out of touch with the product or the product's purpose and culture. I guarantee if we were asked today to design for an anchovy paste company, I'd be having a liberal dose of anchovies on my Colombo's Special tonight and probably some more tomorrow on my toast.

Where did you grow up?

I grew up in a small town in Wyoming called Laramie. I think people from Wyoming aren't afraid of hard work. They also tend to spend a lot of time staring off into the horizon while chewing on a reed of grass.

Hometown: Laramie, Wyoming
Favorite color: Wild Blue Yonder
Favorite font: Chalet
Company: /// massive studios
Job title: Cofounder/Designer
Previous employers: Palmquist Creative, Advertising Design, Mercury Advertising

BENJAMIN BENNETT
Cofounder and Designer
/// massive studios
Bozeman, MT

TopDrawer
/// massive technology

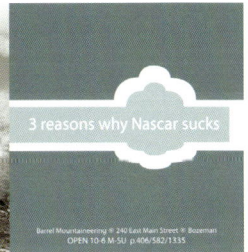

3 reasons why Nascar sucks

barrel with women in mind

pilates, schmilates

barrel with women in mind

Gregg Berryman

Notes on Graphic Design

Gregg Berryman has written many articles on design theory and also contributed to texts on design education. His own books, *Notes on Graphic Design*, *Designing Creative Portfolios* and *Designing Creative Resumes* are used by over 100 universities and sold nation wide. Gregg Berryman's own work has appeared all over the corporate design world. His work has won awards nationally from organizations such as, AIGA, *Package Design* magazine, and the *Creativity* annual.

Where do you work now?
As a Graphic Design professor at California State University.
Where did you work before?
At the Image Group in Chico.
What is your favorite music?
Big Band: Don Ellis, and Gil Evans.
What is the best thing about being involved in design? Simplifying the language of design and working in the niches between the design diciplines.
When did you graduate? Back in 1966 with a MAA.
Where did you grow up? In the town of Butte, Montana!

Designing Creative Portfolios

Designing Creative Resumes

Designing Creative Portfolios
Gregg Berryman

Designing Creative Resumes
A Complete Resource for the Creative Professional
Gregg Berryman

31

Dan Bilyeu
Senior Graphic Designer
International Game Technology
Bozeman, MT

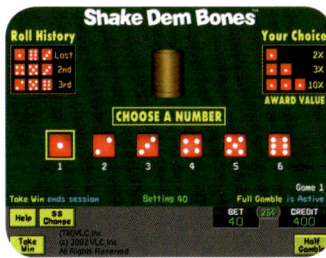

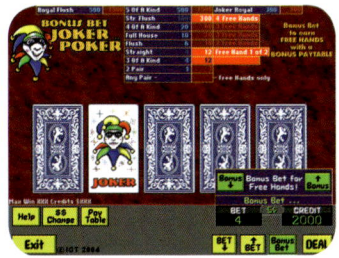

What does your job entail?

I am a Senior Graphic Designer at IGT. I design graphics and layouts for gaming machines.

How does your work vary from machine to machine?

We have machines in many places such as Montana, Las Vegas, Canada, Iceland, and Australia. Different locations have different requirements. Many of our more exciting machines are not legal in Montana; however, anything is possible in Las Vegas. For example, slot machines give me the opportunity to create fun illustrations. People in different areas respond differently to graphics. In Canada, they love hockey graphics, but don't really like cartoon images. So we are constantly doing research to find out what people will want to play.

What kind of research do you do?

I travel a few times a year to play the games. We need to be aware of what games are being played the most and why. The games need to look fun and exciting, but they also have to be easy to play. People do not put their money into a game that is hard to figure out.

What can you tell me about your company?

I started with VLC in 1996. We were purchased by Anchor Gaming of Las Vegas in 2000. In 2002, Anchor was bought by International Game Technology (IGT, the 800-pound Gorilla of the gaming world). IGT is headquartered in Reno, Nevada.

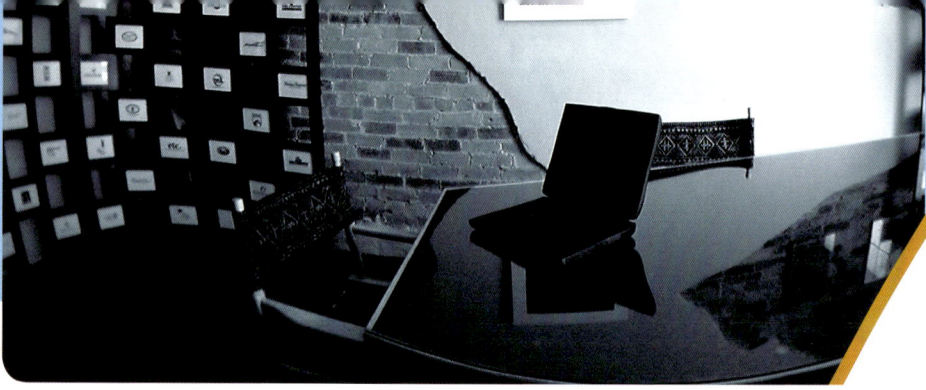

What has the computer done for your style?
It has opened up the time to have unlimited options which in turn requires even more time.

What designer has influenced you the most?
I appreciate the style of designers such as Charles Anderson of Minneapolis and a number of other contemporary designers who build upon an obvious look. However, I try not to have a noticeable "style" or "look" that crosses over from one client to another. I design for the purpose, then create a style specific to the clients' needs, which in turn creates their own unique look and separates them from the crowd.

What advice would you give an aspiring designer?
Never stop looking for good design, everything can be improved upon. No one, client or otherwise, has an unlimited budget or time frame. Mastering your talents will give you the edge to create the most compelling and creative work in the shortest amount of time.

Did you always think you would be in design?
Originally, no! I began in the School of Business at MSU. I took an art class, just for my own interest, and as part of the art class we had to sit in on a Professor presentation. The presentation I chose to go to was a slide show of Anne Garner's graphic design work in LA, designing record covers. The next morning I changed my major and I never looked back!

TUPELO

est. 1995

grille and wine bar

whitefish

Tim Braun

President/Art Director
Fossil Creative
Kalispell, MT

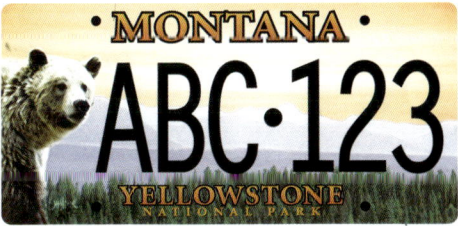

Agua~Terra
HEALTH SPA

Rocky Mountain
AIRCRAFT SERVICES
A division of Rocky Mountain Avionics, Inc.
JET · TURBINE · PROP · AVIONICS

· MONTANA ·
ABC·123
YELLOWSTONE
NATIONAL PARK

· MONTANA ·
ABC·123
Montana Weed Control Association

CHEVROL

· MONTANA ·
ABC·123

35

BILLBROWN
Freelance Illustrator
Seattle, WA

If you could have dinner with three people in history who would they be?
Andy Warhol, Martha Stewart, Alfred Harris

When do you turn down jobs?
Only when I'm too busy, or the product is lame.

What is your advice for future illustrators?
Practice, practice, practice. If you draw, draw every day. Hone and develop your style but let it evolve over time, or you'll have a very brief career. If you want to freelance, don't quit your day job for the first year. I promise you won't be making jack for at least that long. Also, freelancers should consider getting a rep, but choose very carefully. There are some unscrupulous people out there. I suggest meeting or emailing illustrators whose work you admire and getting their advice whenever possible. Bring them gifts!

SPENCER BUCK   DESIGNER K2

K2 SKI MARKETING / INLINE SKATES
vashon island   WASHINGTON

What do you like about being a graphic designer?
Creating something tactile that shows your personal
style and what influences me at the time.

What brought you to MSU and the graphics program?
Close friends in Bozeman, Bridger Bowl, Grateful Dead
album covers, and the Montana mystique. Also failing
to register for classes and needing a studio credit.

What do you miss about Bozeman?
Copious amounts of snow, Bridger Bowl, riding my cruiser
everywhere, The Molly, a bacon and egg on asiago bagel with
provolone at Bagelworks, summers, Ken's special, Bucks run,
rooftop at the Crystal, KGLT, and small town gossip.

How did graphics prepare you for the future?
I was lucky enough to have a design internship which was really
beneficial. Not only for real world portfolio pieces, but also how to interact
with vendors and disgruntled radio station general managers.

What is one of your favorite memories ?
Jeff Conger's epic question to ask oneself when trying to apply vertical type.
"Why am I doing this, why am I doing this, why am I doing this???"
Also an amazing group of people as well as
designers that brought diversity and a lot of laughs.

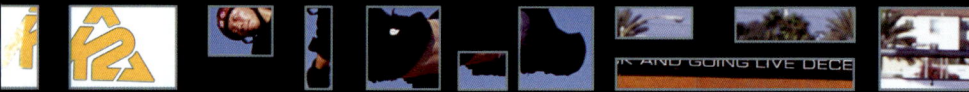

What brought you to K2?

A ferry from west Seattle . . . No, really because I was given a name there, and I have always been a staunch supporter of K2.

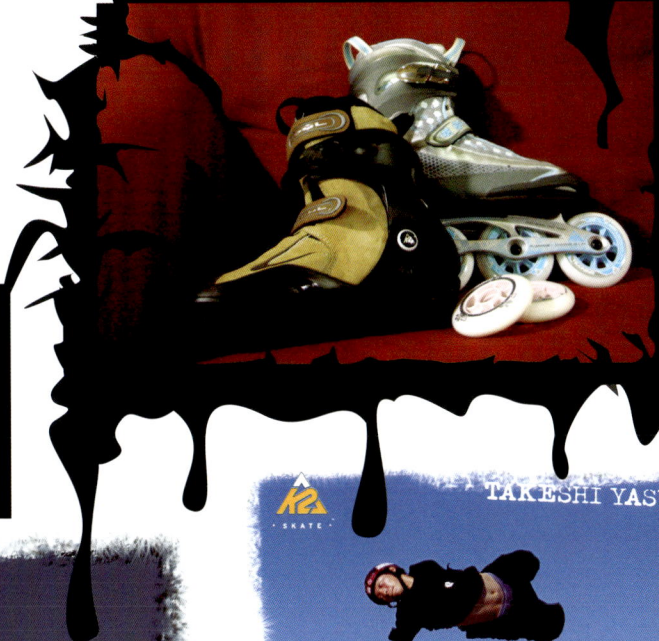

K2 SKATE

TAKESHI YASU

ROLLK2.COM IS BACK AND GOING LIVE DECEMBER 2

Supporting Street and Vert Skaters since 1994

K2

X3

X3 ladies

Scott USA
Snowboard Pipe Gloves
Wintersport Fall 02-03

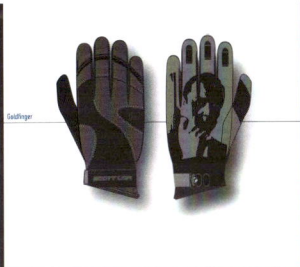

X1

Goldfinger

What is your favorite design style?
White space with bold color.

**What advice do you
have for new designers?**
Graphic design is merely the
spatial relationship between
ideas. Don't let the desire to
create something mind blowing
stop your creativity altogether.
Pressure is helpful when it
motivates, but is detrimental
when it consumes.

Where have you previously designed?
I was an inhouse designer at Dr. Bott
in Portland, Oregon designing
ads, brochures, packaging, etc.

What is your favorite font?
Right now, it is Artista.

Jen Cox • Graphic Designer • Classic Ink • Bozeman, MT

41

JODY NEIL CREASMAN

Publications and Marketing Coordinator
Oregon College of Arts and Crafts
Portland, OR

Jody, where did you grow up?
In the town of Great Falls, Montana!

What is your favorite color and font?
Green is the best! And I like Trade Gothic!

Who were your previous Design Employers?
I worked for Embrosini Design as a Senior Art Director.

Where do you see yourself in five years?
I see myself continuing to work in the educational setting of an art college . I am currently the Publications and Marketing Coordinator for Arts and Crafts in Portland and the job fits me well. I get to wear two hats as both the Creative Director/Designer and PR/Marketing Director. I enjoy the variety of my work and feel that the PR and marketing skills I am acquiring are allowing me to broaden my skill set for future opportunities.

What advice would you give a new designer?
My advice to any designer starting out in the field would be network, network, network. Start out by researching potential firms that may be interested in your type of work. Start emailing or calling these firms and keep an organized list of all the firms you have contacted. If a firm is not hiring at this time try to persuade them to let you come in for an informal informational interview. The more people who look at your portfolio, the better idea you will have of what your strengths and weaknesses are as a designer and even as a potential employee. An informal interview gives you a feel for the firm and its employees and helps you decide if you should keep pursuing the firm as a potential employer.

What time of the year are you most productive?
I don't find that my productivity is seasonal. I seem to work more productively and efficiently when I work on several projects at once. This overlap forces me to stay on task and keep all of the projects on schedule.

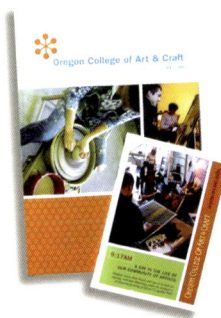

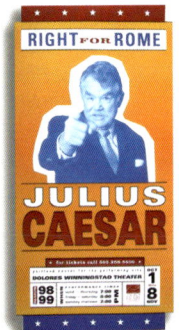

Was designing in the real world what you thought it would be?

There are two things I learned within the first couple of years as a graphic artist in the "real world." First, I had a lot more to learn about people and business in order to consider myself a professional graphic artist. Second, graphic design is not only about using your creativity, it is about having a skill that will get you a job . . . there will be parts you love, and parts you don't love.

When you reach a creative block, what do you do?

Give myself a break - walk to a coffee shop, flip through art & design magazines, organize my workspace, talk to someone.

How did you get your first design job?

I got my first design job about 4 months after I graduated from MSU. I had been in Montana for almost 5 years and wasn't ready to go back to Seattle. I wanted a design job I could live off of easily, and one that my style would fit with perfectly. At the time it was very important to me to find the "perfect" job in "perfect" Montana. I had no idea that place would end up being Dillon, Montana. I saw an ad in the paper for an in-house graphic artist at Great Harvest Franchising. As I read through the job description, I knew it was written for me. Within the next couple of months, I had hand-delivered the 3-page application, had a one-hour phone interview, and then a 3-hour personal interview. I was asked questions such as, "If you were an animal, what kind would you be and why?" It was then I knew for sure their search was over.

Where are you working now?

I started Lucky Girl Designs in January 2004, and I work out of my home. My business includes graphic design and custom greeting cards, invitations, and announcements. I originally included my artwork as a part of my business, but as I do more painting and collage work, I feel like it is a separate entity. I hang art several months out of the year in coffee shops and restaurants.

What is one of the most valuable lessons you've learned?

I've learned to face my mistakes, do what I can to fix them, and most importantly, learn from them.

What is an important skill to acquire?

It is incredibly valuable to have great communication skills.

What is your favorite color?

Green. Green is alive and lush, cozy, free. I am surrounded by so many awesome shades of green where I live - the Evergreen state, the beautiful Northwest. Lucky me.

What advice do you have for aspiring designers?

Stay true to your passion. Be open and honest. Be respectful no matter what the situation, and in return, you will be respected both professionally and personally.

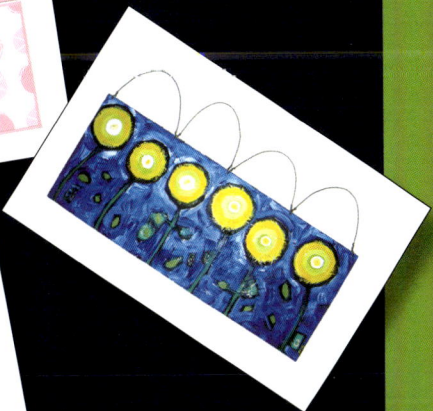

Lucky Girl Designs ™

MONTAQUA ™
Montana Spring Water • Bottled at the Source

William E. Cullen

Freelance Designer
Denver, CO

What three skills contributed most to your success?
First, my communications skills have been critical. If you cannot communicate your ideas, you need to find another profession. Second, sales skills have also been important. You have to be able to sell your ideas to clients. Third, drive. If you are truly driven and you can harness that drive, nothing can stop you.

What would you say your top three design skills are?
Typography , visual continuity and technical ability.

What are some of your favorite hobbies?
My favorite hobbies are restoring my 1975 Jeep CJ-5 and training my dog. I am also very obsessive over Star Wars. It isn't really a hobby, it is more of a life passion.

Your Best Friend In The Accounting Business

HURRY! SALE ENDS MARCH 29, 2002

SAVE 30% - 40% thru March

Is Now Offering Some Tax Season Relief

MANAGEMENT | ACCOUNTING | RELATIONSHIP

ᗡuniLink

Custom KINGPIN
LONGBOARDS ★ BOZEMAN, MT

Nat Cundy
Graphic Designer
King Design
Bozeman, MT

When did you get your first skateboard?
Way back in Junior High.

How did you get into skateboard design and why?
I grew up skating and riding BMX bikes. I had the first skateboard in my group of friends. I've always enjoyed hands on work and making stuff. I also grew up in a machine shop that my dad ran.

What are your favorite skateboard wheels?
Kryptonics.

What kind of truck do you own?
I just bought an old faded red shop truck, a '57 Ford ... Jeff Conger won't let me paint it.

Where did you grow up?
In beautiful Lakeside, Montana!

Do you have any advice you would give to a new designer?
Don't be afraid to do things you haven't done before.

Do you feel the MSU design department prepared you for life as a designer?
Yes, they taught me to have a good work ethic and lots of personal style.

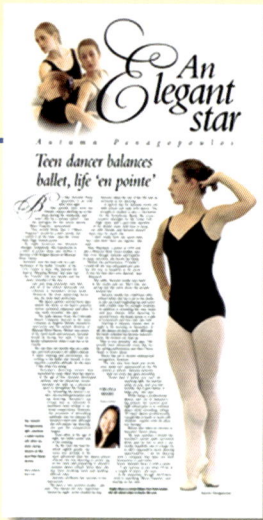

What are the ups and downs of newspaper design?

Newspaper work is fast-paced and always changing. In a word . . . exciting. It is very challenging because you have to deal with an overabundance of content and a limited amount of space. This is especially true of a small paper like The Great Falls Tribune. Unless you have a dayside job, like feature writers or management, you need to work odd hours, usually 3:00 p.m. to midnight. I am a night person so I actually enjoy it.

What did you envision yourself doing after you graduated?

Like most people I graduated with, I imagined I would most likely be working at an advertising agency.

What is some advice you could offer to design students?

Just realize there are plenty of applications for design out there, not just ad design. Keep your eyes and options open and you will find a field that suits you.

NICK DANIELS

Graphic Designer ■ Great Falls Tribune ■ Great Falls, MT

craig davidson
designer / owner

Civic Design
Minneapolis, Minnesota

How did you end up in Minneapolis?
The short version of the story is that a number
of things happened at once. I was working at
Rick Valicenti studios in Chicago when he
decided he wanted to take his studio in a
different direction. In the new scenario I would
be a partner with Rick and another designer
from the studio. Around the same time, I
recicieved a phone call from the head designer
at Walker Art Center. She remembered me from
when I interviewed with her in New York for a
different design position at the museum. It was
pure coincidence that these two events occurred
together. I wasn't financially ready to be a partner
with anyone and was looking for a reason to take
a break from Chicago. They offered me a job at the
Walker Art Center and I moved a couple of
months later.

What is the most fulfilling aspect of your job?
When an idea, or project, has been simmering
in my head for a while and when I actually sit
down to work it out visually and it all clicks!

Who has influenced you over the years?
Marge, Dave, Oscar, Jill, Harold, David, April,
Armin, Bradbury, Lester, Wolfgang, Hamid,
Tom, Anton, Malcom, Rick, Jeenee, Seeley,
i.e . . . everything.

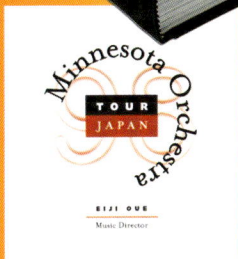

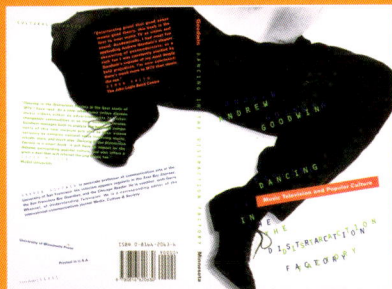

korey doll

Director/Designer

Edwards Design

Burbank, CA

Your favorite city?
Cooke City, Montana!
Why? The population is
only around 140 people.
All of that aside, Cooke
City is simply in an
amazing spot. You have
Yellowstone Park and
the Beartooth Mountain
Range, two of the most
unique locations one can
find. If I could somehow
live there, I would.
Favorite sport? Baseball.
Favorite color? Blue.
Hometown?
Billings, Montana!
Favorite rock bands?
Bad Brains, Fugazi, etc.
**Any previous design
employers?** Ikon, Billings
Gazette, Creative Domain.

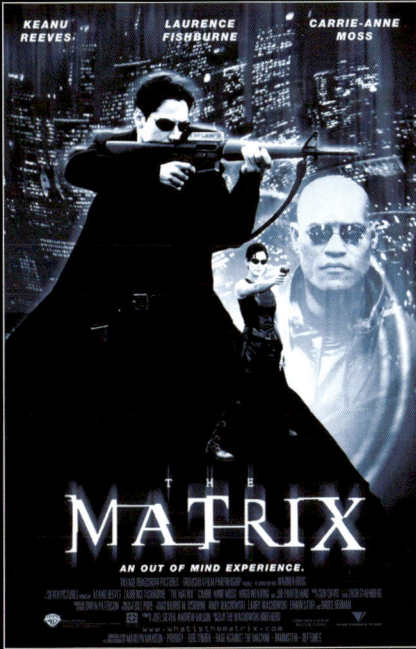
KEANU REEVES   LAURENCE FISHBURNE   CARRIE-ANNE MOSS

THE MATRIX

AN OUT OF MIND EXPERIENCE.

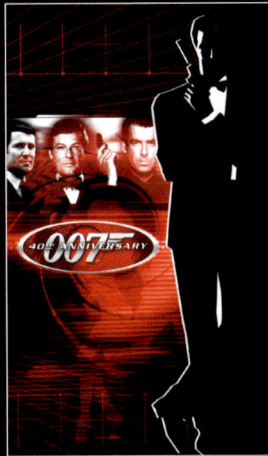
40th ANNIVERSARY
007

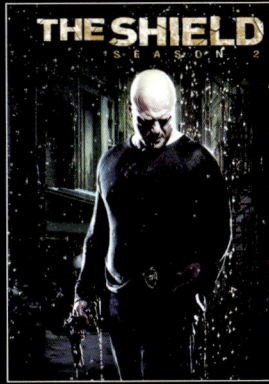
THE SHIELD
SEASON 2

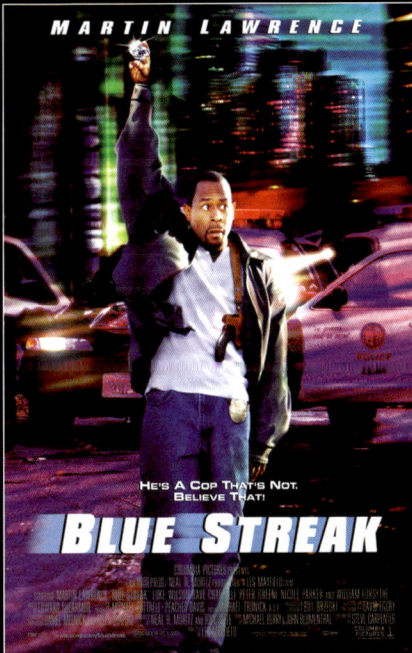
MARTIN LAWRENCE

HE'S A COP THAT'S NOT. BELIEVE THAT!

BLUE STREAK

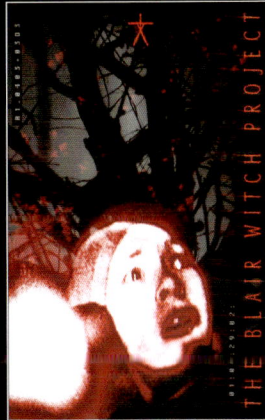
THE BLAIR WITCH PROJECT

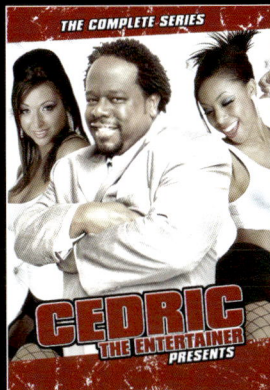
THE COMPLETE SERIES

CEDRIC
THE ENTERTAINER
PRESENTS

55

KRISTEN DRUMHELLER
Montana State University
Office of Communication and Public Affairs
Art Director

WHERE DID YOU GROW UP?
I grew up here in the beautiful Gallatin Valley, close
to Bridger Bowl.

WHAT ADVICE WOULD YOU GIVE TO GRADUATING
SENIORS ABOUT THE GRAPHIC DESIGN JOB MARKET?
Show as much variety in your portfolio as possible.
When we hire designers, we're not only looking for the
flashy full-color showcases of your design talent, but
also nuts-and-bolts work like formatting large blocks of
text and creating charts and graphs.

WHAT ARE THE BENEFITS OF BEING A GRAPHIC
DESIGNER IN BOZEMAN AS OPPOSED TO A LARGE CITY?
It's possible to achieve a better balance between having
a challenging career in design and enjoying the other
important parts of your life: spending time in the
outdoors, raising a family in a great place and being
part of a close-knit community.

WHAT ARE YOUR FAVORITE STRESS RELEASES?
Rock climbing and skiing.

WHAT IS YOUR FAVORITE RESTAURANT?
Columbo's Pizza in Bozeman!

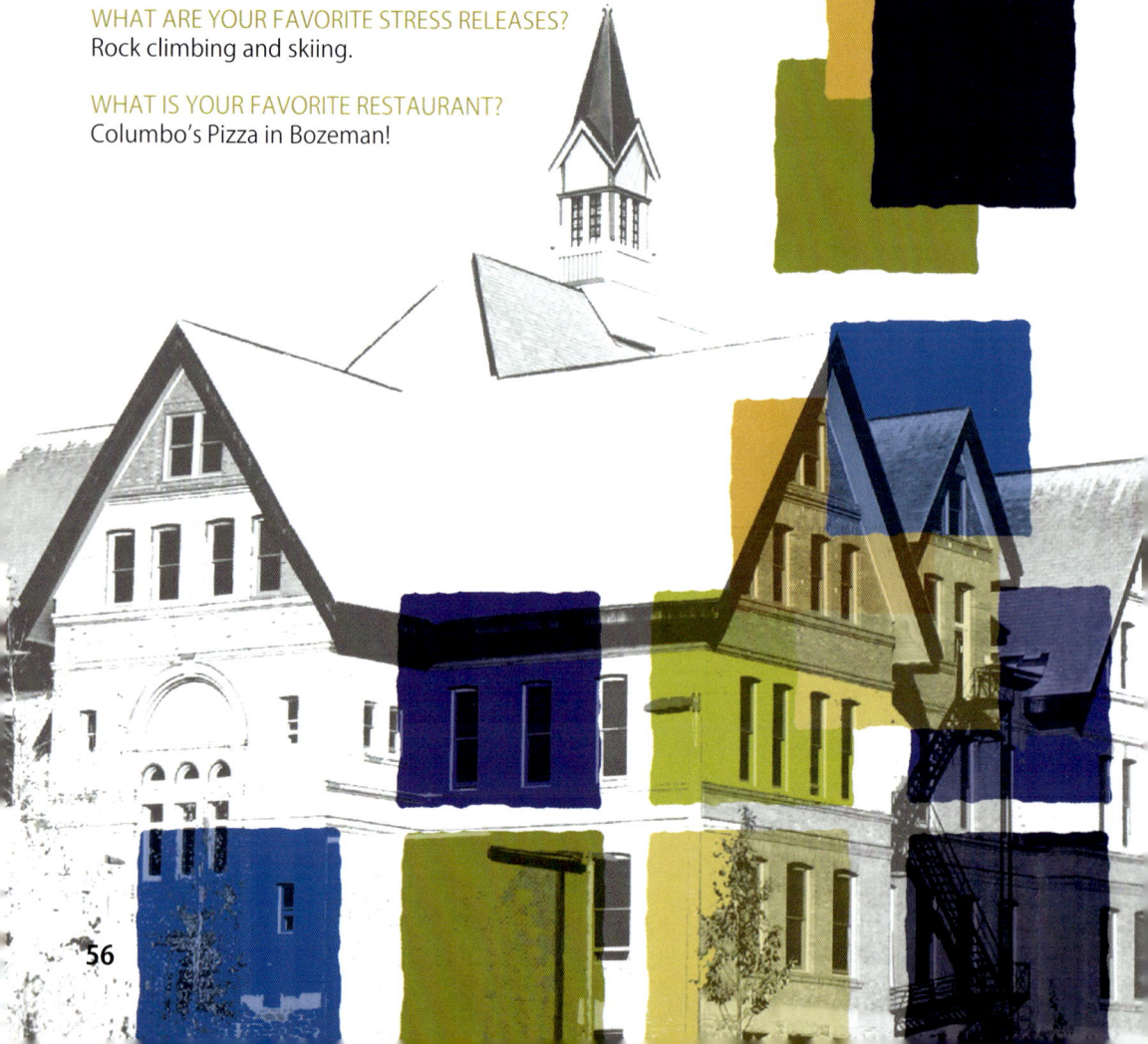

cross pollination
OF A
M O N O C H R O M A T I C
tone...

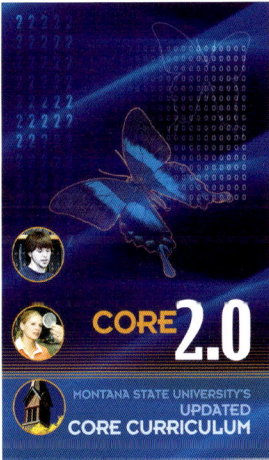

CORE 2.0

MONTANA STATE UNIVERSITY'S
UPDATED
CORE CURRICULUM

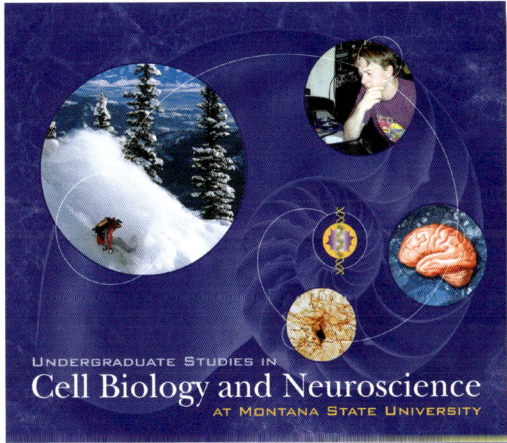

UNDERGRADUATE STUDIES IN
Cell Biology and Neuroscience
AT MONTANA STATE UNIVERSITY

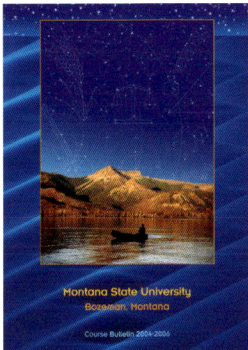

Montana State University
Bozeman, Montana

Course Bulletin 2004-2006

WE CAN RIDE IT!

SKÜRTZENDIRT

Assistant Vice President, Corporate Web Development   Nomura   New York, NY

How is living in New York?

Certainly working across from the World Trade Center taught me that just when you get settled, everything can change. I think people who live in New York are passionate about it because it gives you a feeling like you survived a battle. As though you struggle so hard you have something that not everyone has. It's not for everyone, that's for sure.

Any words of wisdom?

Keep it simple, study the foundation of great design, try both outstanding visual design and minimal information design. Draw inspiration from the world as you view it, not just from the latest style trend. If you're in web design, consider taking computer science, logic, programming courses as well. The world is about saturated with flash designers.

Future plans in the art world?

My future includes building a web-based application called smatter.tv. It should be launched in the summer of 2005. It is designed as an application to deliver high quality multimedia content over the web to large format plasma/lcd screens. Sort of like choosing your own wall art for the next generation of web enabled screens (TV) and other large displays like digital signs. I want to build applications that present digital art content, as I see a huge area of potential in the emerging digital art arena.

What is it like working for Nomura?

I had to learn to look for opportunities where others weren't looking. By persistence and determination and a lot of very hard work, I won the right to redesign the entire corporate intranet, which extended to thousands of pages and hundreds of business applications. I would give several personal pitches to the CEO and many other department heads on a daily basis. Convincing them that not only could the web make their business more profitable, it could also be more attractive. On Wall Street you have to relate everything to money first.

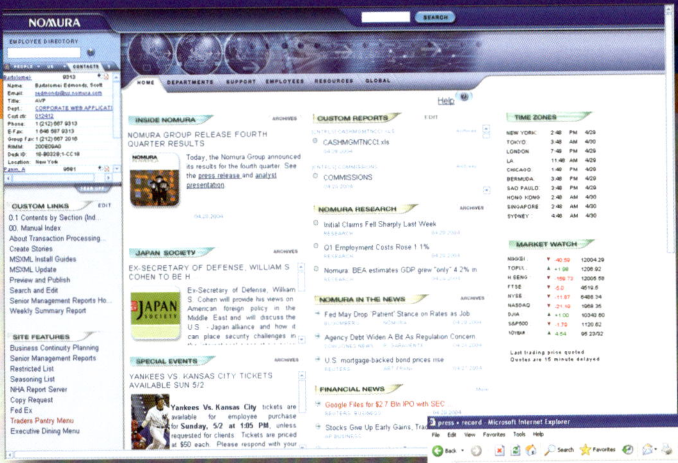
NOMURA
INSIDE NOMURA
NOMURA GROUP RELEASE FOURTH QUARTER RESULTS
CUSTOM REPORTS
TIME ZONES
NOMURA RESEARCH
JAPAN SOCIETY
MARKET WATCH
NOMURA IN THE NEWS
SPECIAL EVENTS
YANKEES VS. KANSAS CITY TICKETS AVAILABLE SUN 5/2
FINANCIAL NEWS
CUSTOM LINKS
SITE FEATURES

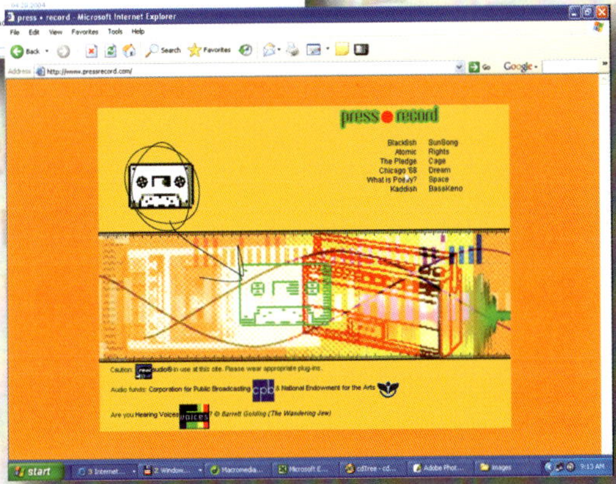
press + record - Microsoft Internet Explorer
press record

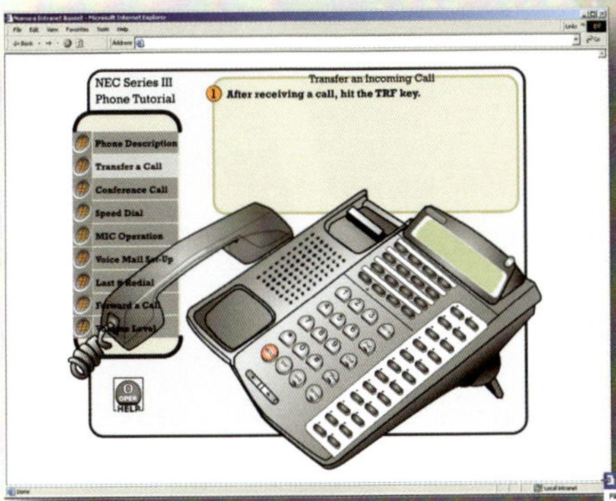
NEC Series III Phone Tutorial
Transfer an Incoming Call
After receiving a call, hit the TRF key.
Phone Description
Transfer a Call
Conference Call
Speed Dial
MIC Operation

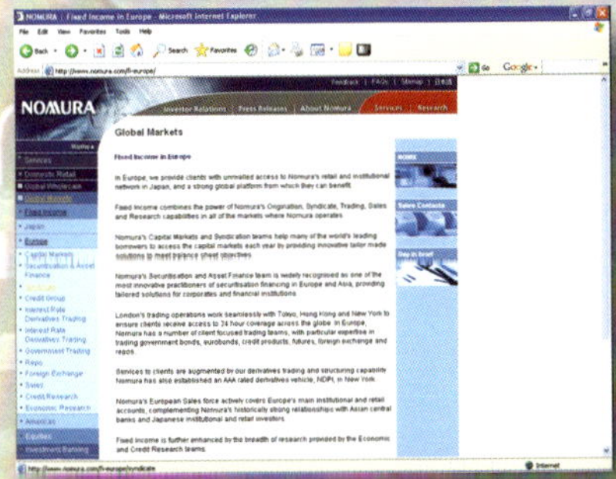
NOMURA
Global Markets

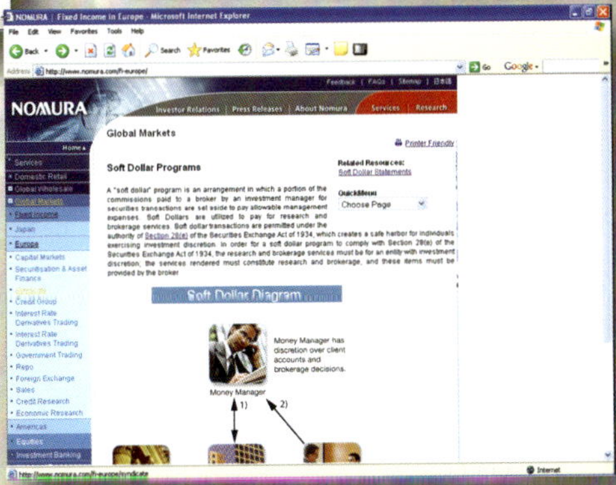
NOMURA | Fixed Income in Europe - Microsoft Internet Explorer
NOMURA
Global Markets
Soft Dollar Programs
Soft Dollar Diagram
Money Manager

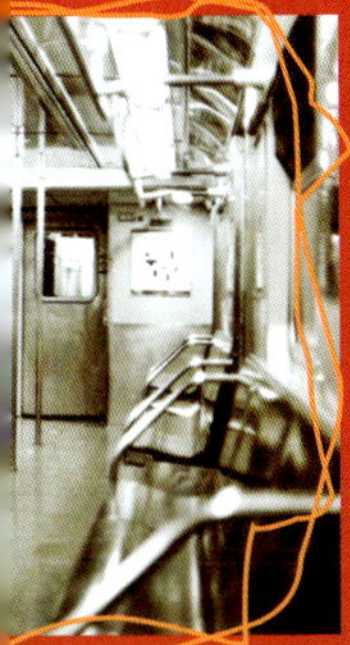

SOY CHEESE
PATE
SMOKED FISH
EXTRA SHARP CANADIAN CHEDDAR
ENGLISH SAGE DERBY
JOAN OF ARC
ITALIAN BALSAMIC VINEGAR
IMPORTED ITALIAN PROSCIUTTO DI PARMA
FONTINA VALDOSTANA
CREAMY ITALIAN DOLCE LATTE GORGONZOLA
NATURAL TURKEY BREAST
IMPORTED ITALIAN GNOCCHI
SMOKED SEBASTIAN
FRESH PESTO
MARINATED DANISH FETA

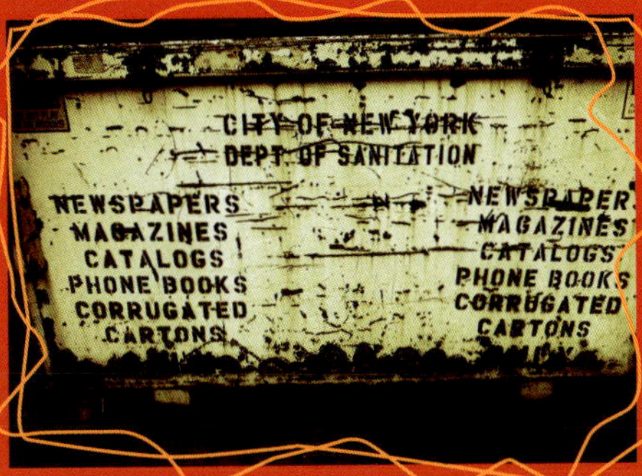
CITY OF NEW YORK
DEPT. OF SANITATION
NEWSPAPERS
MAGAZINES
CATALOGS
PHONE BOOKS
CORRUGATED
CARTONS
NEWSPAPERS
MAGAZINES
CATALOGS
PHONE BOOKS
CORRUGATED
CARTONS

MARY EDWARDS
Graphic Designer
Murdoch's
Bozeman, MT

Where do you get inspiration from?
Everywhere . . . a supermarket, a gas
station, a post card in the mail,
pop art, fine art, magazines,
and everything in nature.

Where did you grow up?
Absarokee and Reedpoint!

**Do you have any advice for
upcoming designers?**
Know WHAT you want and WHERE
you want to be. You may end up there
longer than you expected. Also, be firm when
you negotiate your salary. Yearly raises do not impact
your earnings as much as a good up-front negotiation.

How was your transition from student to professional designer?
I feel like it was a natural progression. I started working at Big R, now called Murdoch's as a
full-time designer while I was still attending Montana State University. Once I graduated,
I continued to design for the corporation. After a year or so, I was placed in charge of
advertising and was able to hire my own crew of designers. It was quite the challenge,
but I obtained an amazing team that I am still working with.

What is the difference between hay and straw?
Hay is a feed product made from alfalfa and straw
is a by-product of wheat which is used for bedding.

MURDOCH'S
RANCH & HOME SUPPLY
Garden Center

blue water
T a s k   F o r c e
Gallatin Watershed

carto-logic GIS

Bring the whole family,
even the dog.

An Invitation Only Event.

Carhartt

We're here to answer any
questions you have
about Clothing, Tools, Animal Nutrition, and more!

We'll even feed your herd!

Bozeman
HOT
Springs
spa & fitness center

Robyn Egloff

Art Director
Mercury Advertising
Bozeman, MT

What keeps you motivated?
Seeing really good design.
When I see a TV commercial
or a new ad in a magazine
that is really creative, it
makes me want to create
something that good.

**Where do you look for
inspiration ?** We have a
lot of trade publications
in the office archive:
Communication Arts, Print,
etc., that help a lot when
I'm in a design rut. They
also help me to keep up
with what's going on in the
advertising and design world.

How did you go about landing your job with Mercury? I started dropping my resume off at
different places around town. I also met with a few people on the list to just show my portfolio
and get to know people. After a week or so of not getting any calls back, I was getting a little
frustrated until I got a call from Jamie here at Mercury. I came in to show her my book (which
was a black box with my art mounted on black boards, very simple and inexpensive) They
started me part time, and after about three months I started full time.

What does your work primarily consist of? A lot of time is spent concepting. Once we
get some ideas nailed down we begin with the design. We don't do a lot of photography
or illustration in house but we will art direct when we are using photographers and
illustrators. There is also a lot of production work to do. Once you come up with the ideas,
they have to be executed. I really like the concepting part of projects, figuring out the best
way to communicate the product or service to best reach the markets.

What advice would you have for graduates? Keep an open mind while looking for work.
Graphic design is such a broad field, something that doesn't seem like much of a "design" job
might turn out to be. Keep things simple. Let your book represent you but don't be afraid to be
confident about yourself. Companies want to hire a good fit, not just the best book out there.

What has been your most rewarding project? Bozeman Library Foundation

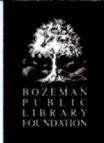

Matthew
Grimes

Graphic Designer
Info Space
Seattle, WA

What is the best part of being a designer?

I enjoy the initial exploration and concepting of a project. You never know where you will end up, but the journey is always interesting.

Do you have any advice for aspiring design students?

If you know what area of design you want to focus on, go there. Put yourself around those people, companies, or places that will allow you to do what interests you most. Be patient with yourself and with your growth as a designer. If you keep going you will become more and more confident and versed as a designer and that will only lead to greater opportunities.

Where do you see yourself in ten years?

Hopefully, not sitting in front of the computer all day! I hope that I can get back to some of the more fine art related things that I like such as painting, printmaking and illustration. Mainly, I want what everyone else wants, to be healthy and happy with where I'm at in my life.

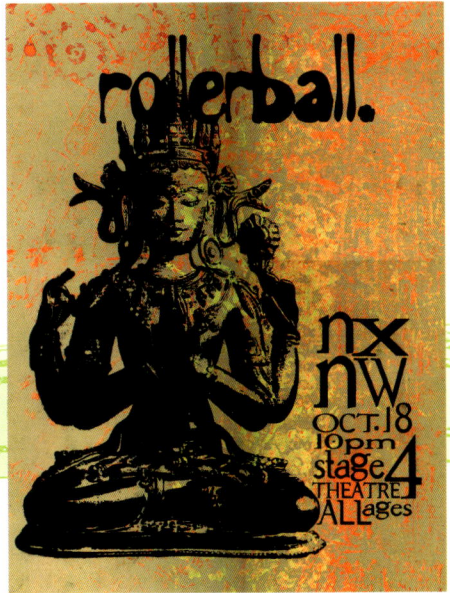

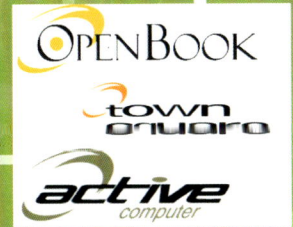

What do you enjoy most about working in the design industry? Working for myself.

What is best about living in California? The weather, the ocean, clubs, parties and art galleries.

Who is your favorite star to design clothes for? Jennifer Aniston!

What is the latest fashion fad? Vintage rock T's that are replicas of original tour shirts are everywhere, denim and t-shirts are here to stay!

What is your favorite band? The Stills

Who have you worked for in the past? I worked for MTV, as stylist and designer for MTV Movie Awards and Singled Out.

Blaine Halvorson

Junk Food, Inc.   Co-owner/Designer   Venice, California

"I actually started designing clothes while I was still in the design program at MSU. I worked at a screen print shop at the time so after work I just started making t-shirts and hats. I then began getting into the more high end fashion, actually designing dresses and suits. My initial work while in Bozeman is what got me out to Los Angeles and into the whole fashion scene. I started designing clothes for MTV movie awards and also doing stage outfits for a bunch of different rock bands. I was actually partying more than working, which was fine because I met a ton of people. These contacts I made socializing turned out to be an important part of business. Once I actually moved to LA I got back into the t-shirt end of apparel and that is where I have stayed. Without the celebrities wearing your product it is difficult to get to that next point, so having that access really helped my company succeed and grow at a much faster pace than most other apparel companies. I feel I know and understand the fashion market well, so I keep my focus there, plus everyone always needs a new t-shirt!"

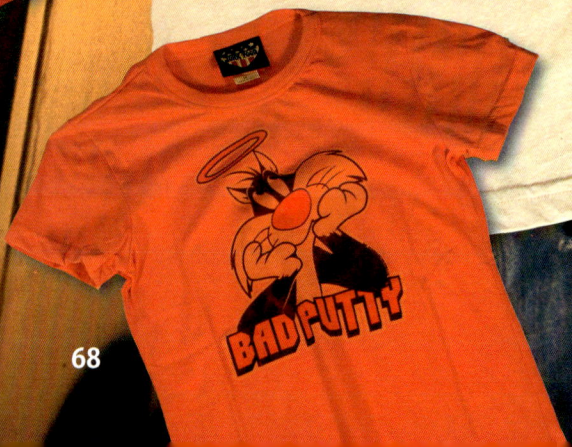

Today Junk Food is considered the most influential licensing company in the world, currently shipping more than 1,000,000 shirts a week to top retailers around the globe. With the largest collection of licensed brands of any apparel company, Junk Food creates trend-setting shirts for such visual giants as DC Comics, Sesame Street and Warner Brothers. They whip up memorable artwork for the dynamic Wonder Woman, loveable Oscar along with Tweety and one bad putty tat. Worn by top celebrities, its shirts have been seen on Justin Timberlake, Christina Aguilera, and Jennifer Aniston making it one of Inc. magazine's top 500 companies this year. Pushing beyond the retail racks of Macy's, JC Pennys and Hot Topic, Junkfood is proud to open it's first retail stores in Japan this fall.

Adam Karig Haynes
Apparel Graphic Designer
Adidas
Portland, OR

1
adidas
TMAC

IN LOVING MEMORY
JMJ 1965-2002

Road to Apollo

Garnett

70

Where are you working now and what is your job title?
I work for Adidas in Portland, Oregon and my business card says "Apparel Graphic Designer."

What would you say your top three skills are?
Illustration, attention to detail, and a broad style range.

What three skills contribute to your success?
I work well with others, I work hard, and I am accountable for my actions.

How would someone go about getting a job like yours?
Move to Portland, get a job, and plan on the process taking awhile. Corporations have a lot of people involved with everything, and the process can be maddeningly slow. But with persistence, I have seen it pay off many a time.

What kind of experience should be sought after?
Learn about screen printing and what sort of design works best for printing on fabric. Starting your own small company and selling tees is really good experience. There are a lot of folks applying for jobs at these companies, so do anything you can to set yourself apart.

Who are some of your previous design employers?
I worked at SUB Graphics at MSU before moving to Portland and getting the position with Adidas.

dave HEBERT

Evergreen Aviation
McMinnville, OR
Graphic Designer

What sort of work did you do for Evergreen Aviation?
I worked in the in-house art department. They have a variety of divisions to design for, including aviation cargo, sales and leasing, helicopter services and agriculture divisions. This required designing brochures, logos, advertisements, billboards, and material for trade shows.

What are you currently doing?
After experiencing several years of the world of corporate design with Evergreen Aviation, I recently decided to return to Montana.

72

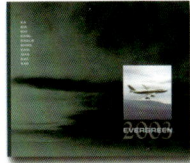

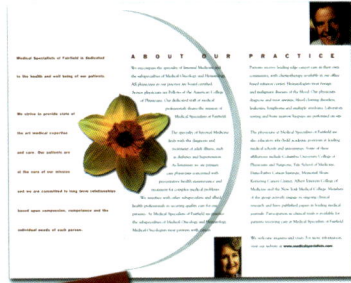

What design work did you do immediately out of school?
Freelance, mostly logos and brochures.

Where did you grow up?
Madison, Connecticut, a 20 minute trip away from New York City. The music, style, and people of the area have had a lasting influence on my design.

Why did you choose MSU?
I was drawn by the mountains, and started school studying ecology. After taking the "Design 101" course I decided to switch my major to graphic design.

CARL HEIDLE
Art Director
Quisenberry Marketing
and Design
Spokane, WA

How do you relate design to everyday life?

I relate it to everyday life very well. I don't feel like I have a job in design, I have a life in design. Most of my friends are in my industry and I spend much of my time at work-related functions. People often envy graphic designers for having a creative job in a very loose and fun environment, and they should. Being in advertising and design has a certain Hollywood element to it that attracts some of the most outrageous, hilarious, and otherwise psychotic people to the business. I can guarantee that as a designer, the stories you will tell in the retirement home will be far more exciting than those of the typical nine to five crowd.

How does a designer stand out?

Good designers have integrity and heart. They know what good design is and will fight for it. To be a great designer, however, one must not lose sight of the purpose of the piece they are creating. Graphic design is communication. If your piece fails to communicate accurately or effectively, it is useless, regardless of how beautiful it is. When issues arise, the best will not be frustrated. Instead, they will use the confines and challenges of a given project to create clever, elegant, and unexpected solutions.

Are the colors you see the colors you get?

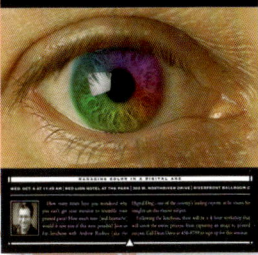

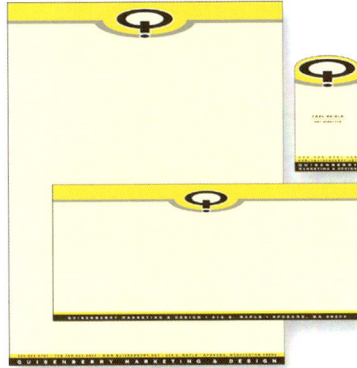

5 WAYS TO CAMP WITH KOA

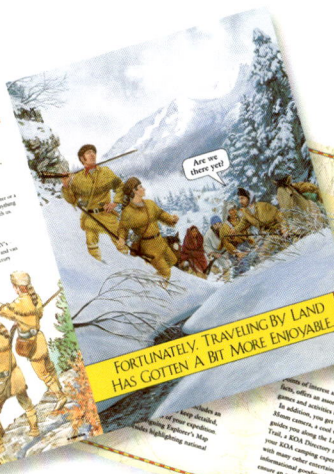

FORTUNATELY, TRAVELING BY LAND HAS GOTTEN A BIT MORE ENJOYABLE.

Are we there yet!

SHOULD YOU PRICE YOUR HOME HIGHER
IN HOPES OF NETTING
THE MOST PROFIT?
OR LOWER IN HOPES OF MAKING
A QUICK SALE?

Skyhawks

ERIC HEIDLE

WENDT ADVERTISING   ASSOCIATE CREATIVE DIRECTOR   GREAT FALLS, MT

A Little History: I graduated in 1992, and ever since I've earned a living "drawing pictures," as my grandfather would say. I've also done some teaching for MSU and the University of Great Falls, passing on Photoshop skills to the next generation. When I'm not in front of the computer, I'm in the mountains somewhere, reading a topographic map upside down.

Where Do You Look For Inspiration? Design annuals always remind you how high the bar is set. Beyond that, the more ideas you scribble down on paper, the better your work will be.

How Did You Get Where You Are Today? Hard work, a bit of luck and the Gaussian Blur filter.

What Was Your Most Rewarding Project? Creating a state-wide anti-smoking campaign paid for with the tobacco companies' own cash.

What Advice Do You Have For Future Graduates? Spend some time learning what you don't want to do before you take a job.

Where do you draw inspiration from?

From life, mostly! I used to look through design books and pull from those, but recently I found more inspiration from, say, subway art. I went to New York and ended up shooting pictures of anything pasted to a wall that caught my eye.

What do you like most about your workday?

I like producing the work most of all. The first few hours of pure creativity make the whole part of being a Graphic Designer worthwhile. You can call yourself an artist and still make a living. Taking a large volume of visual research and sitting down and putting it into something that is your own voice . . . that's what I like.

Who are your mentors?

War photographers.
Journalists.
And Vonnegut!

Why did you become a designer?

I needed a way to make a living, and was raised under an artist's roof and understood and employed the process. I was at a friend's wedding once and his uncle turned to me and said, " If you're not an artist you've failed." While designers are still commercial artists first, there is still some amount of freedom in a world of factory assembly lines.

What are your aspirations for Bootleg?

To create a network of support for clients that need both marketing and advertising solutions. When my partner Byron DeVries and I sit in meetings, we generally tell clients that their profit is our first concern and everything else stems from that. I see Bootleg slowly expanding with a heavy creative base and solid logistical expertise.

the Bay
BAR & GRILLE
Lunch

APPETIZERS

APPETIZERS

The next best thing to floating in the
Sea of Cortez with dolphins
the Bay
BAR & GRILLE
Lunch & Dinner
Full Service Bar
Casino
Gallatin Valley Mall, Bozeman
406-587-0484

Where do you get your inspiration for design?

For inspiration I use that immense satisfaction that comes with absolutely nailing a project. It motivates me when I'm feeling uninspired. Also I've been using music a lot in my conceptual process. The music sends its own imagery and color into the mix, and keeps me fluid enough that I don't get stuck on one idea. I quickly jot down and sketch every idea and image that makes even the briefest appearance.

Any advice for designers entering the job market?

Stay excited. It's easy to get bored and stagnant. If you're bored with the work, your portfolio will likely be boring. Network!!! In the job market a personal referral from someone you know will get you through a door much faster than your resumé or portfolio. Learn all you can about printing: prepress, ink, presses, bindery, etc. Learn to bid out a job.

Who have you worked for?

Amazon.com
Memphis Radio Kings
Tamarac

Where did you grow up?

The big "B" - you know Billings!

Do you have a favorite artist?

Mike Mignola and Derek Hess.

DANIELLE HURD
Owner/Designer
Studio 1212
Boise, ID

Studio
12 · 12

Tell me about Boise!
We have plenty of work.
With quite an array of firms
and freelancers, the spectrum
runs from cheap and dirty to
elaborate, high dollar design.
Competition is definitely present
in this town, but many businesses
look for work from companies
that would be a good fit for them.

Advice for aspiring graphic designers?
I'd have to pass on and second the advice
that Jeff Conger gave my class. That is, pair your
graphic design with a hobby or something you love.
If you like the outdoors, look at working for a non-profit
group that maintains trails or climbing areas. If you like
motorcycles, see about working for a Harley magazine or become
a freelancer and solicit work from people in that industry. It will keep you
interested in what you are doing and connected with the people you enjoy.

TWO RIVERS

Boise Traffic

Bluebird Yoga

Peaceful Belly Farm

Patrick Jeske

Designer/Partner
co-operate design co.
Bozeman, MT

digisphere

nm

What advice would you give to an upcoming designer?

Examine everything and work hard. I guess that kind of goes without saying. Look for inspiration in unlikely places.

What is the best part of being a designer?

I find satisfaction in the entire process, beginning with early conceptualization to the final solution.

Who were your previous employers?

Charles S. Anderson and Adidas.

What was the hardest part of starting your own company?

It has been difficult adjusting to the geographical differences that currently exist between my partners and myself.

What project in school had the biggest impact?

I guess it would have been my senior thesis. Applying the principles and fundamentals of what I learned during my course of study, while developing my own direction, was an invaluable experience.

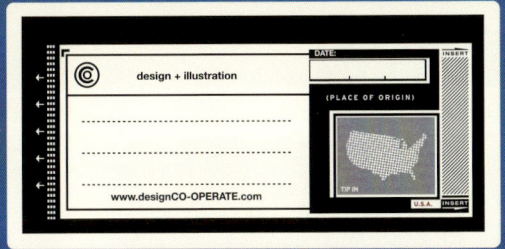

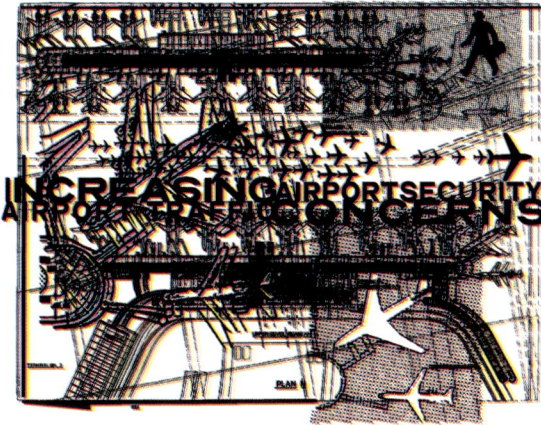

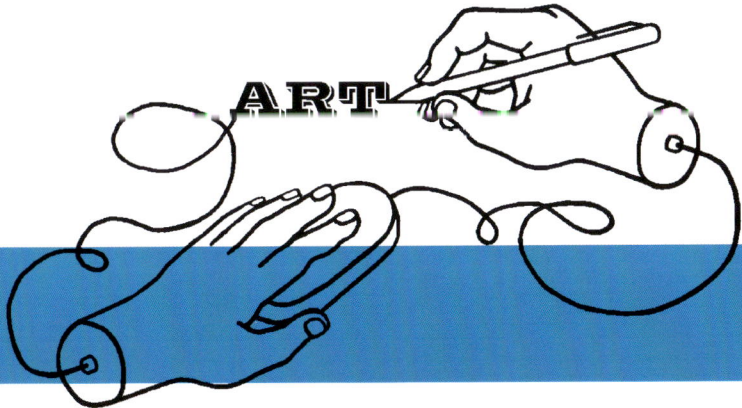

JASON JOHNSON
Freelance
Bozeman, MT

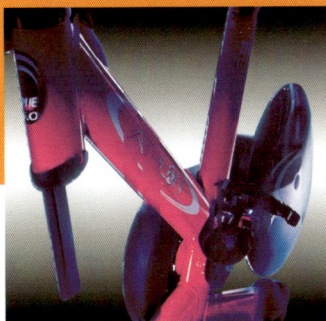

What advice do you have for designers?
Do your homework on marketing and business skills, keep up your design-related network of people and most of all, travel and experience new things as much as possible. Nothing refreshes the design spirit better than getting away from it for a short period of time and witnessing what happens in the rest of the world. Take a lot of photos while you are at it.

Who are some of your previous design employers? Nike, StrategixID, and Morrison Creative Company.

What is your favorite aspect of design? Its ever-changing nature. There is always something, like technology, that changes the field, and there is always someone out there who seems to push the field along, too. With wireless and laptops, it's possible to work almost anywhere, so you can go to some place that inspires you to get what you need to get done, done. The evolution of design and all it encompasses has been an amazing thing to try and follow, much less keep up with.

What is your favorite font? A favorite font . . . you can't go wrong with classics like Univers and Perpetua. It all depends on the use. I have more that I dislike than I can think of that I like. For example Papyrus!

Where did you grow up? Great Falls, Montana. The amazing G-FUNK!

What is one of the most valuable lessons you've learned? Time management, and the fact that I am basically miserable with the concept. This comes into play when you are quoting a job, when you are working on a job, and when you need to meet the requirements of the client. I did a job that was printed in Hong Kong, where any changes required a three day turnaround.

RUSS KAISER
Freelance 3-D Modeler
Bozeman, MT

WHERE DID YOUR INTEREST IN 3-D MODELING DERIVE FROM?
My interest came from video games and movies.

WHAT IS YOUR FAVORITE STAR WARS MOVIE?
The Empire Strikes Back!

WHAT ADVICE WOULD YOU GIVE TO GRADUATING SENIORS ABOUT THE DESIGN FIELD?
If you plan on doing freelance work try to get to know other freelance artists around you.

WHAT ARE THE BENEFITS OF LIVING IN BOZEMAN AS OPPOSED TO STARTING A CAREER IN A LARGE CITY?
Thanks to the internet I really don't think it makes much of a difference anymore.

WHAT DID YOU PUT IN YOUR PORTFOLIO THAT YOU ARE MOST PROUD OF?
My final poster for *Star Wars Insider* magazine.

WHERE ARE YOU FROM?
I grew up in Billings!

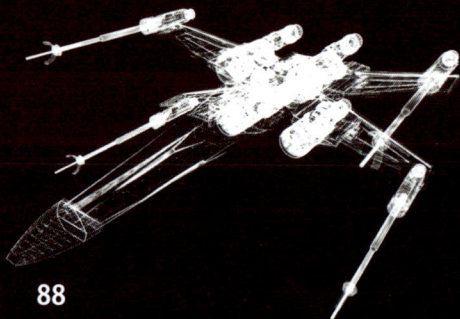

Inside the Insider
Number 43
Features
28 BRIAN BLESSED: A BLESSED EVENT
52 GEORGE LUCAS INTERVIEW PART TWO
56 DROIDS OF EPISODE I
64 DECIPHER: THE THRILL OF VICTORY
66 LUCASFILM LIFERS
Departments
8 REBEL RUMBLINGS
10 PREQUEL UPDATE
22 PREQUEL PROFILE
24 STAR NEWS
62 IN THE STAR WARS UNIVERSE
72 STRAIGHT FROM THE HORSE'S MOUTH
76 SCOUTING THE GALAXY
82 THE LAST PAGE
THE WONDER COLUMN
ON THE COVER
from the editor's desk
"IT IS YOUR DESTINY"
Somebody asked me the other day how long I had been doing this job. I said I'd been working here for five years. But actually, as you can see from the photo below, that's a lie—I've been working on being a Star Wars fan since I was eight years old. Managing editor Scott Chernoff has been hard at work being a fan almost as long—but I beat him 'cause I'm older by three years.
JON SNYDER
SCOTT CHERNOFF
JON BRADLEY SNYDER
STAR WARS INSIDER 7

Insider 45
Departments
from the editor's desk
THE CULT OF STAR WARS?

Insider
from the editor's desk
We'll Miss You, Jack

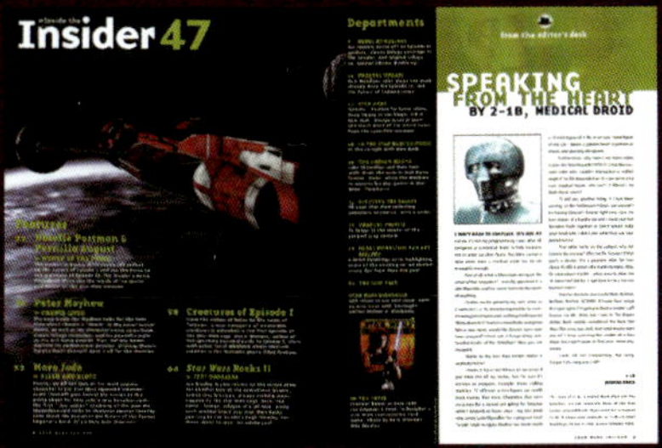

Insider 47
Departments
from the editor's desk
SPEAKING FROM THE HEART
BY 2-1B, MEDICAL DROID

Kris Krieg

Creative Director
Vivify
Austin, TX

What have you found to be one the most important aspects of design?

I've found that a strong grasp of type can help in many situations. Your projects always looks better when you understand how type works. You can also use type as a crutch, when clients don't have a budget for art work, you can make a strong design with type alone.

How did you get to where you are today?

I graduated in 1995 and then traveled the states interviewing with various firms. I found an interest in environmental graphics and signage. I established Vivify as a one man shop in Austin, Texas and have run it for the past six years.

List of Clients:

The Lady Bird Johnson Wildflower Center
American Red Cross of Central Texas
Samsung Semiconductor of Austin
Webber+Hanzlick Architecture
Jimmy Jacobs Custom Homes
Junior League of Austin
Velocity Credit Union
Mueller Law Offices
Texas Appleseed
Regent Digital

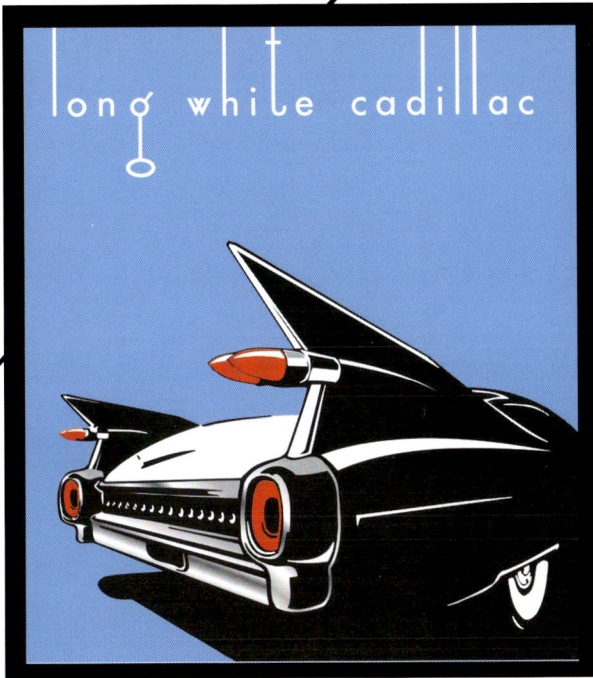

long white cadillac

AIN'T THAT LONELY YET

BAKERSFIELD BISCUITS
THEY'RE YUMMY!

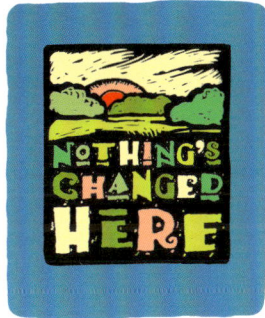

NOTHING'S CHANGED HERE

KING OF FOOLS

TURN IT ON, TURN IT UP, TURN ME LOOSE

WHAT'S THE MOST INTERESTING BOOK YOU'VE READ LATELY? *Running with the Bulls* by Valerie Hemingway. **WHY?** Inspiration to travel, read, draw, and keep a journal.

IF YOU WEREN'T A DESIGNER WHAT WOULD YOU BE? Something physical, entertaining and crazy - Cirque Du Soleil trapeze artist or Bandaloop dancer.

WHICH ASPECT OF DESIGN MOST INTERESTS YOU? Making a meaningful idea possible.

WHAT ARE YOU UP TO LATELY? Museums, publications, architecture, and signage.

ANY REAL ADVICE? Travel, read, draw, and keep a journal!

FAVORITE COLORS? Red, yellow, blue!

Barbara Kuhr is a parner in the design firm Plunkett+Kuhr. In 1992, she and her husband, John Plunkett helped found Wired magazine, launched HotWired, the world's first commercial site in 1994 and the search engine HotBot in 1995. For seven years, before selling the company, Plunkett + Kuhr telecommuted to Wired's San Francisco offices from their design studio in Park City, Utah. Recent design projects include a signage system for the Louvre, yearly exhibits for Carnegie Hall and graphics for the Sundance Film Festival.

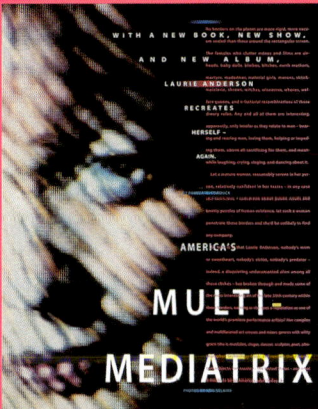

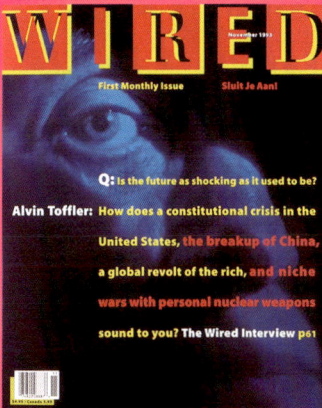

93

Mary Kysar

Art Director
makelike design
Portland, OR

How was "makelike" founded? My friend Topher and I had been talking about it for a while. We were asked to fly to New York and interview to design a new magazine. We got the job and wrote our respective letters of resignation on the plane home. makelike was born.

Where do you look for inspiration? I look to books and magazines. I really like this bookstore in Portland that exclusively carries old periodicals all the way back to the 1800's; it's a great place to go for inspiration. For illustration, I just take a walk with my camera and get lots of close up shots of plants, trees and grasses and start drawing from those photos.

What has been your most rewarding project? *Milk* magazine

Describe your ideal design project: A project that I start working on from the beginning. The budget is big enough to produce it correctly. Everyone working on it is excited about it. It doesn't last longer than a month.

What advice would you have for graduates? Keep at it! It's hard to get that first job but it gets easier after you have a little experience. I got my first design job (at Johnson and Wolverton) by accident. Right out of school I talked to lots of design firms and sent out lots of resumes with no luck. I waited tables and bartended for a year. While I was doing that I would make posters for fun and post them all over Portland. Hal Wolverton saw one of those posters and asked me to come in with my book. They had just started doing *Raygun* magazine and were looking for a few designers to help out. I worked on that issue and waited tables at night. After that, they asked me to come on staff.

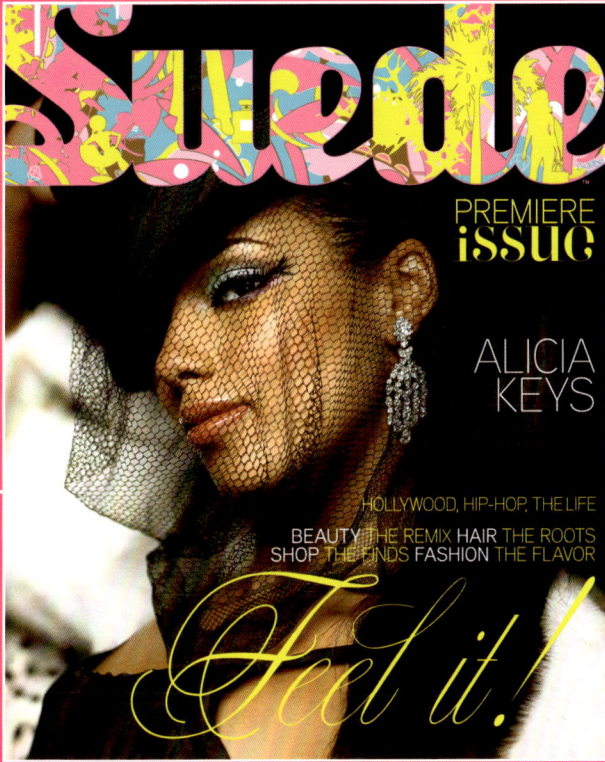

Suede

PREMIERE
ISSUE

ALICIA KEYS

HOLLYWOOD, HIP-HOP, THE LIFE

BEAUTY THE REMIX HAIR THE ROOTS
SHOP THE FINDS FASHION THE FLAVOR

Feel it!

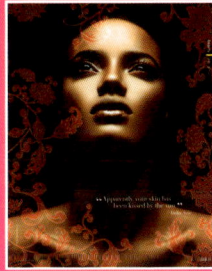

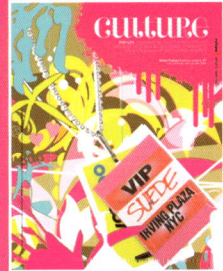

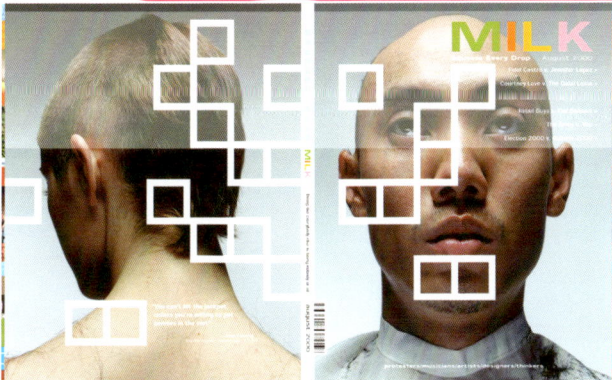

Claude

Rebekah Lane

Graphic Designer
Nintendo of America
Redmond, WA

How did you land your current job?
Another alumni, Jill, was already working for a company that contracts to Nintendo. She recommended me. I went to an interview with my kooky plastic toaster portfolio that I had created in school. They eventually hired me as a contractor, then when someone else quit, I was right there, ready to take the job. Basically, I was extremely persistent, and not embarrassed to be a little weird.

What does your work primarily consist of?
Layout is the biggest part of my job. I work on a magazine and players' guides.

What advice would you have for graduates?
Don't underestimate the value of any knowledge you may have on things that are not directly related to design. I have found that knowledge of pop culture, current music and trends to be extremely valuable to my position. About portfolios, be sure it reflects your personality. I know for a fact that one of the big reasons I was hired was my personality and how they thought I would fit into the group.

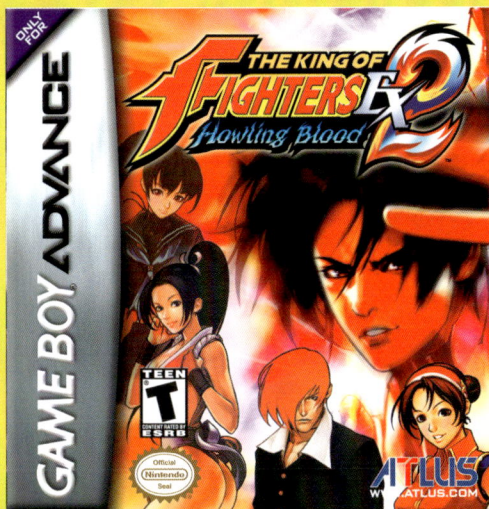

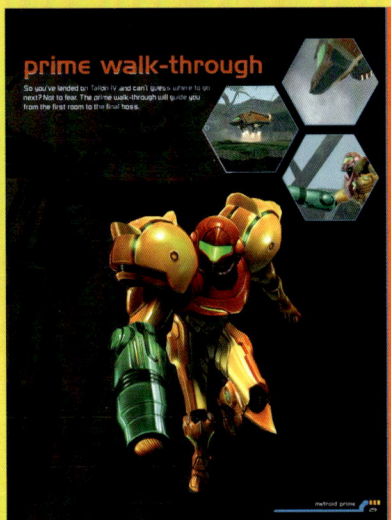

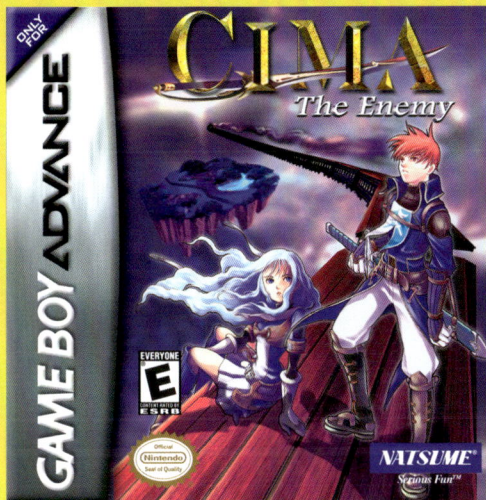

Jill Anderson-Story
Graphic Designer
V-Design Inc.
Redmond, WA

What are your creative influences?
Posters and Rave fliers. I love the work of
Swiss graphic design firm, Büro Destruct.

Where have you worked previously? This is my first job out of college. Before I graduated, I designed ads for the ASMSU Exponent, and did an internship with the Theodore Roosevelt Medora Foundation.

What was your most rewarding project? My wedding invitation. It was great having people wonder if I made them or bought them.

How did you land your current job? At the library, I sifted through newspapers of the cities I was willing to move to. I found this job through the Seattle classifieds.

What advice would you have for graduates? Start thinking about your resumé early. Try to do volunteer design projects, competitions or internships. These things can be added to the "work experience" on your resumé, and will give you an edge after graduation.

97

Heidi Lauman

What advice would you give to an aspiring designer?
Get as much real-world experience as you can, even if you're still in school. For example, with print design: get experience with taking a project from start to finish, from initial concept through production and then to a print shop. And be confident (but not inflexible). A client will trust your opinion and support your design ideas when you show that you have confidence in your work.

What got you interested in graphic design?
I always knew I wanted to work in a visual or creative field. As a youngster, I was obsessed with logos and photos in magazines. It wasn't until my second year of college that I decided to pursue the specific field of Graphic Design.

Who is your current employer?
I am currently working as a freelancer from my home office, specializing in logo design and illustration. In October of 2003, I came to the realization that I no longer wanted to sell my creative soul to rich men in suits. I have been successfully freelancing ever since.

What do you enjoy most about your job?
The most satisfying aspect of my work is the occasional, but always desired, "Aha!" experience when I create a concept that is solid and visually compelling. Ultimately, when the client says, "Yes! That concept is perfect!". The fact that I am my own boss and work from home is quite satisfying.

Who are some of your favorite artists/designers?
Some of my favorite artists include contemporary illustrators like Henrik Drescher, Lane Smith, Sara Midda, Jane Ray, Michael Schwab and Cathleen Toelke. I'm also fond of the artists Francoise Gilot, Alexander Calder, Frida Kahlo and Amedeo Modigliani.

What are some of your hobbies and passions?
Food, food, food! Books, films, and jewelry making.

Home Town:
Born and raised in Soda Springs, Idaho!

TUCKER
CONSULTING

FOUNDATION
HOME LENDING

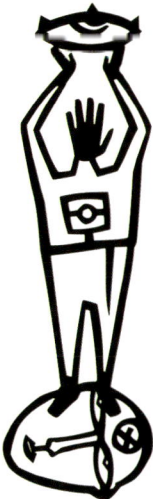

99

Nichole Lear

**Principal and
Graphic Designer
45 Degrees North
Bozeman, MT**

What kind of firm is 45 Degrees North?

45 Degrees North provides integrated solutions for its clients across print, multimedia, brand, advertising and marketing media.

Was it hard starting your own business?

Self employment is probably one of the hardest things you can choose to do, but also one of the most rewarding. The first two to three years were very tough and required nearly every waking minute of my time to build the business. If you can make it through the initial start-up phase, after that every year is better and more rewarding than the last.

How do you advertise for your company?

We have had great luck with word-of-mouth advertising; happy clients are always your best form of advertisement. Other than that, we do a variety of self promotion, from sponsorship of local events to advertisements and focused direct mail. We also have a great website that has been a useful advertising tool.

Where's the farthest you've traveled to take pictures for a client?

James and I traveled to Cabo San Lucas to do photography for a Mexico themed clothing catalog.

IN ESSENCE
SALON · STUDIO

"I WANT TO MAKE BANKING FIT MY SCHEDULE"

We're that Good.

YELLOWSTONE BASIN BANK

Yellowstone
CUSTOM COUNTRY HOMES

Custom Timber Frames | Handcrafted Log Homes | Custom Frame Homes

Howard Mills 406-842-5068 | www.bigskybuilders.com

ENNIS
on the Madison
FLY FISHING
FESTIVAL
SEPT 3-6 2004

Wild River Adventures
GLACIER RIVER
JOURNEYS

EXPERIENCE THE
RIVER WILD
with
WILD RIVER
ADVENTURES

FISH, HIKE OR JUST RELAX!

DELUXE LOG LODGES · RUSTIC CABINS · BOAT & CANOE RENTALS

wedge
Wilderness Edge Retreat
CLIFF LAKE, MT

1-866-226-7668 · WWW.WEDGERETREAT.COM

ENNIS
on the Madison
FLY FISHING
FESTIVAL

DANA LYTLE
Planet Propaganda
Creative Director / Cofounder
Madison, WI

Is there one product, tool or gadget that you cannot live without?
I think you would need at least a music machine of some sort? I could throw most of it, (computer, email) away and still be fine. I think I would actually be better.

What have you learned on your own?
Lots of lessons, some more painful than others. Here are a few: Design is a business. Failure is OK. Just don't repeat the same mistake twice. Relationships are key to doing great work. In fact, relationships are more important than the actual work. Don't get too big for your britches. Seek out new clients when you're busy, don't wait until you're slow. Oh and, "Hi, I'm an award-winning creative" is not an effective pickup line!

When did you realize you wanted to become a graphic designer?
It's hard to say because design wasn't my first choice. In Montana, where I grew up, all the kids wanted to be long-haul truckers. There's a diesel truck driving school right outside Madison and I think about that every time I drive past it.

What's the best piece of advice you could offer someone thinking about becoming a designer?
You know that super-critical inner voice, the one "positive thinkers" always say you should ignore? Don't ignore it. It's your best friend!

FLUFF

A definitive guide

1/4 Tattoo Printing

2/4 Scholastic Screening

3/4 Mimeograph

4/4 Turin Process

FLU
FFI
SEL

ATTENTION

WE INTERRUPT THIS
PAPER PROMOTION
FOR SOME RATIONAL THOUGHT.

MOHAWK

"If you gaze for long into the abyss, the abyss gazes also into ..."
—Friedrich

"The solution, eyes into it Rather, with conviction. that you will find the truly fluffy."

DARLING!

It's a pleasure welcoming you to Lynn and Alfred's home, *Ten Chimneys.*
Step back in time with us.

EXPERIENCE KATHARINE HEPBURN'S
DAZE OF WONDER

SHARE CAROL CHANNING'S FEELING OF
GOING TO HEAVEN

DELIGHT IN LAURENCE OLIVIER'S
BELOVED CELESTIALS

Like you, the Lunts' friends escaped busy worlds to retreat to Ten Chimneys.
You will find that friends leave Ten Chimneys always too soon, but always just.
Do let us know if you need anything special to make your visit just perfect.

YOU KNOW LYNN & ALFRED, DON'T YOU

VISIT "ALFRED LUNT AND LYNN FONTANNE: A LIFE ON STAGE"

Enter a bygone era of drama and sophistication as you step through the
façade of the LUNT FONTANNE THEATRE. You can easily envision Alfred Lunt and
Lynn Fontanne, "the greatest acting couple in theatre history," on stage in
their lavish Broadway landmark.

Ah, but perhaps you'd like to direct? Try your hand at six of the Lunts'
productions in the MINIATURE THEATRES, each with its own unique
mechanization. (Alfred adored miniature theatres... you will too.)

Maybe you yearn for the FOOTLIGHTS? Well, just step onstage. You will find
there is so much to know about the artistic legacy of Lynn Fontanne and
Alfred Lunt.

Ah, but you, you should be in PICTURES. You will want to pose as a very
celestial Lynn or Alfred.

What about a sneak peek backstage? Come relax in the Lunts' private
DRESSING ROOM. No one will be the wiser if you rummage through their
dressing table drawers, watch their home movies, or even peep into their
travel trunk. What could be more delightful?

*"It is a very rare thing that two people are equally attractive,
equally talented, equally skillful, and equally devoted."*
SIR JOHN GIELGUD

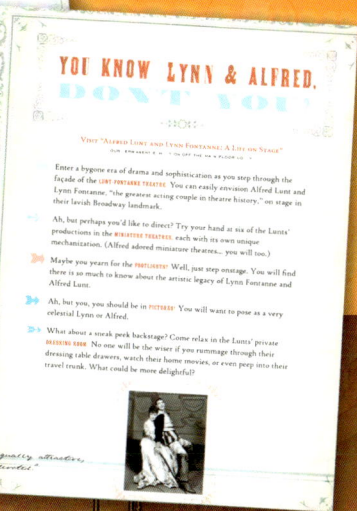

MADISON, WI
★ PLANET PROPAGANDA

Based in **Madison, WI,**
Planet Propaganda is an all-media
kind of machine. Regardless of the
communication channel, though,
they strongly believe that the medium
is not the message - the message is the
message. Whether you want to grab
people by the throat or have them lay
their throat in your hand, the challenge
is the same: Keep the message clear.
Keep the medium transparent.
Be interesting!

PLANETARY SYSTEMS
PACKAGED ENERGY SOLUTIONS

Kakoii Mono

gobuild
KITCHENS, BATHS, INTERIORS

WEST YELLOWSTONE
PUBLIC LIBRARY

THE CLINTONS BAND

ANGIE MANGELS
Lead Interactive Designer
Earthtalk Studios
Bozeman, MT

What are the pros and cons of interactive design?

The pros of interactive design are that the projects are truly interactive and the designer is integral in setting up how the project works and flows between screens and activities. It's really a challenge in figuring out how to organize and present a client's product or story over the web or on a cd-rom in a way that is easy for the viewer to use, and yet still be creative in its presentation. The cons are how limiting the technology can be in integrating and using really cool and interesting concepts, and the limited amount of fonts that we have available to us for use on websites. Another problem is how many people there are out there that are still using old computers and systems and can't view the latest technologies. We always have to keep in mind the lowest common denominators and design our projects so that they work on any kind of system.

What is your ideal design project?

My ideal project is one that has a large budget, an interesting and engaging topic, and an open and trusting client. The more interactive and educational a project is, the more fun we can have in setting it up.

How did you get involved with web design and what makes you keep doing it?

I got involved in web design kind of by accident. I was looking for an internship after I graduated from school and ended up at Earthtalk Studios which is a multimedia company that creates websites, cd-roms, and video. The more I learned about designing for the web, the more I enjoyed it. I like the challenges and variety that is inherent in trying to design websites and in creating a product that is both useful and aesthetically pleasing.

What is the best part about being a graphic designer?

I think the best part is the variety of companies and types of projects that I get to work with. No two projects are ever the same and all require such different solutions and levels of creativity. I really enjoy the fact that I get to learn a lot about these different companies and their projects.

MATT MEEKS

Creative Director / CEO
Moo Interactive, Inc.
Denver, CO

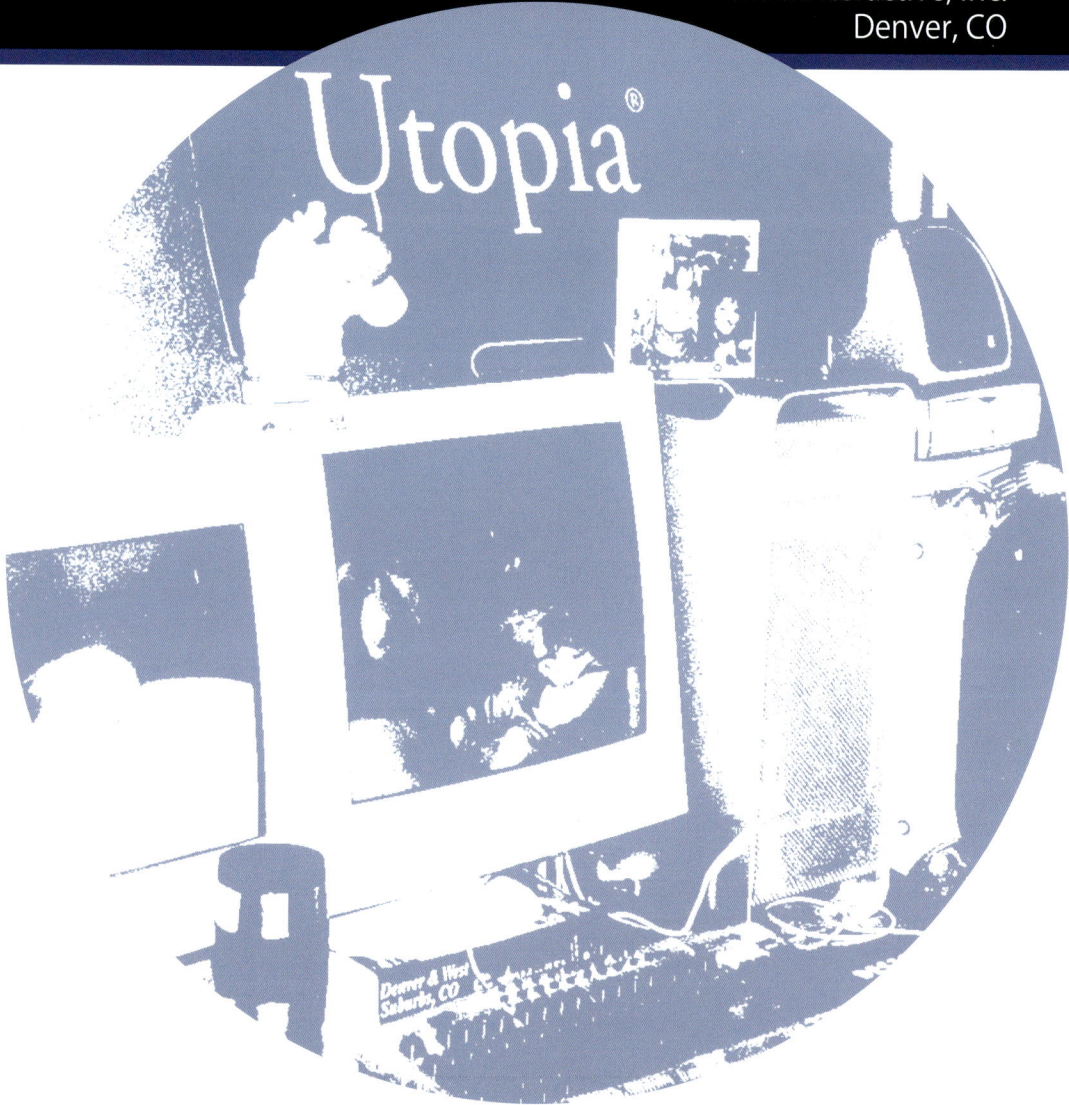

Exchange**Builders**™

What advice do you have for young designers?
Never stop learning, and avoid developing a style. Design for the client, the project, and the audience.

What is one of the most valuable lessons you've learned?
Really listen to your clients. Solutions are always contained within the problem, and understanding your clients' needs will get you most of the way to a solution.

Who are some of your previous design employers?
Barker Design, Mark Mock Design, D3 Agency, and I spent some time as a senior in-house designer with Global Healthcare Exchange.

Where are you working now?
I own my own company - Moo Interactive, Inc. in Denver, Colorado.

How does designing in the real world compare to what you thought it would be?
It's a lot less like "art" and a lot more like "business." The creativity is still very important, but to most clients, it's less important than meeting deadlines and budget.

What is your favorite aspect of design?
Learning about the client, their industry, their audience, their message, and turning that into a creative solution. I love to learn, and working for a variety of clients gives me the opportunity to learn about many different things.

TEK & Consulting, Inc.

Raelene MERCER

Founder and designer
Sublime_miami
Miami Beach FL

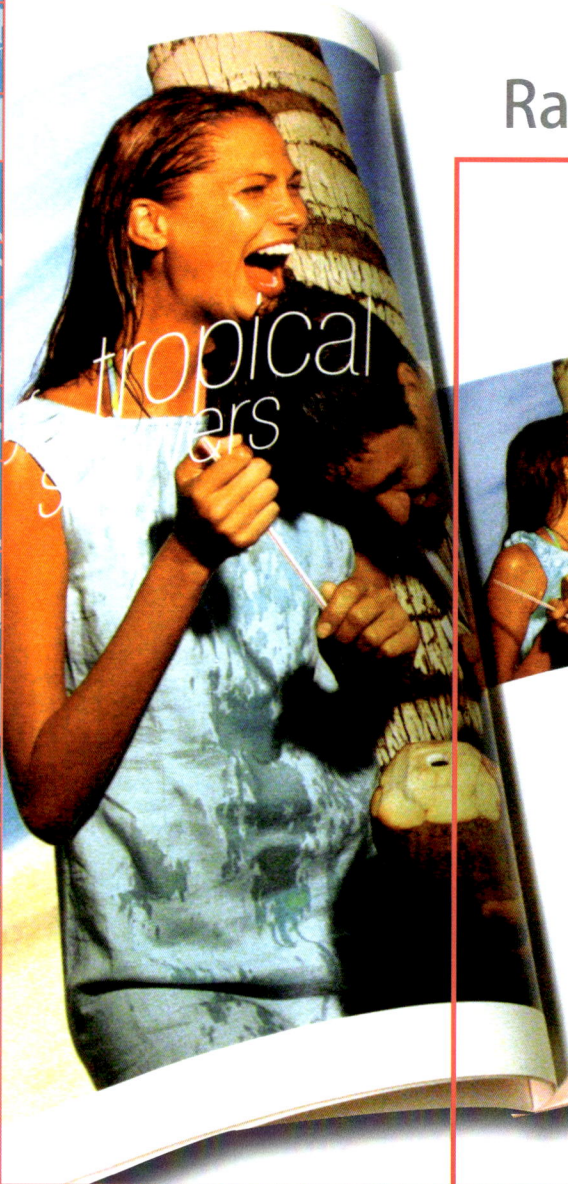

What is rewarding about graphic design and what you do with it?

The constant learning of a variety of industries, the interaction of people from all walks of life and then seeing the results from producing creative marketing solutions.

What is your favorite medium to work with?

Either colored pencil or oil paints. My goal is to begin painting and illustrating again; although I'm so busy with work now that I'm more proficient on a Mac.

Where did you grow up?

I was raised in Miles City, MT. But spent a lot of time at my grandparents ranch in Powderville, MT.

Who are some of your past employers?

I have worked at Pensaré in D.C., Planet Propaganda in Madison WI, Pinkhaus in Miami, and two years ago I founded and became creative director of Sublime Miami.

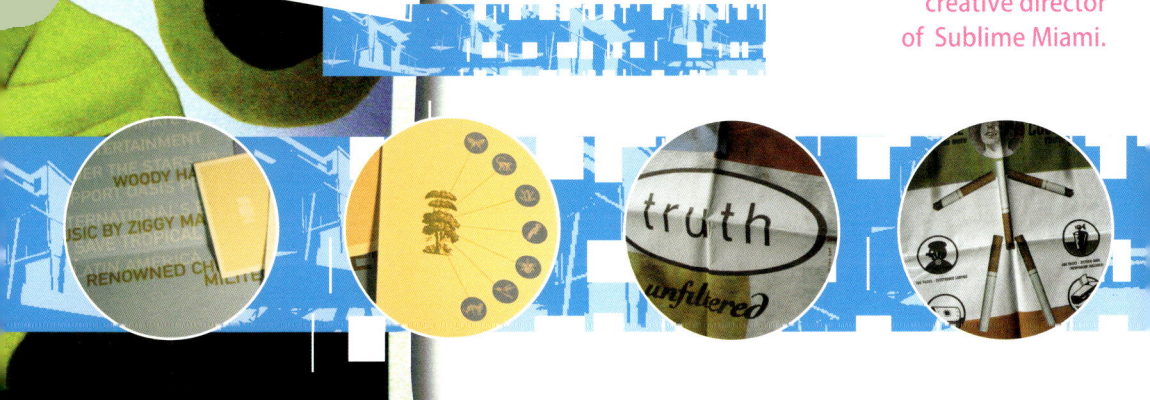

What's an off the wall job you've worked on lately?

A month and a half long food photoshoot for Sunbeam. The aromas in the studio went from scrumptious to fume-city.

ROBERT MERCER
Senior Designer
Starbucks Coffee
Seattle, WA

What's the advantage to working in-house?
Not having to worry about losing clients
brings the stress level down, which
in turn, can improve the overall
atmosphere of the workplace.

Advice for upcoming graphic designers?
Chin up, chin up.

What inspires you?
Doing design that either informs and/or
makes an emotional connection.

Any fine art specialties?
Right after school I focused on
painting for about a year,
then that got traded for music.
In the end, music is my fine art.

Other hobbies?
Rebuilding old 50's and 60's
tube Hi-Fi and guitar amps,
and hanging out with my son.

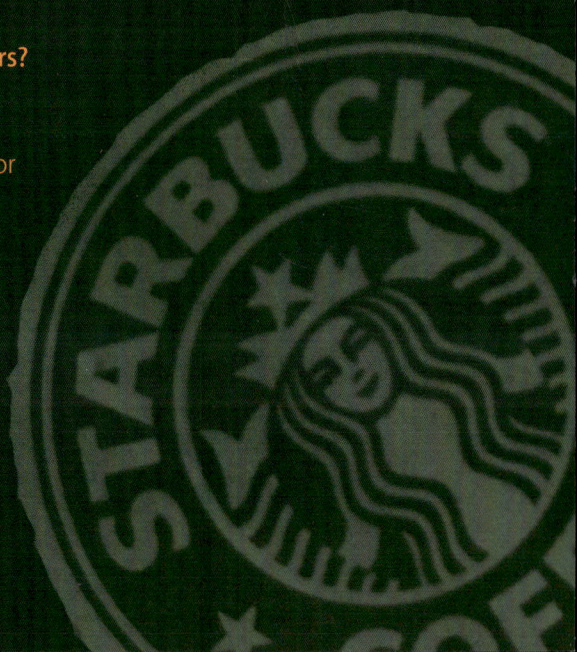

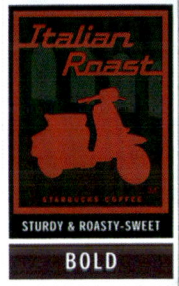

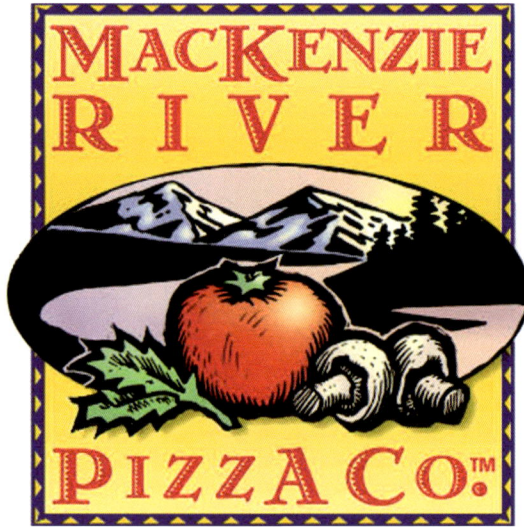

MacKenzie River Pizza Co.™

Stark Raven
CYCLES

Montana Ale Works

Kenyon Noble
READY MIX

MOLLY a. MERICA
Merica Design
Bozeman, MT

Who are your heroes or hobbies?
ANNE GARNER IS MY HERO.
SHE SAW THROUGH MY DESULTORY WAYS
AND GAVE ME A CHANCE AND WITH THAT
FOSTERING CAME THE CONFIDENCE TO
PURSUE A GRAPHIC DESIGN CAREER. SHE
IS AN INCREDIBLE WOMAN AND TEACHER
AND I FEEL SO FORTUNATE TO HAVE BEEN
UNDER HER TUTELAGE. ANNE IS DEFINITELY
ONE OF THE FIVE MOST INFLUENTIAL
PEOPLE I'VE ENCOUNTERED IN MY LIFE.

I DON'T HAVE TIME FOR A HOBBY.

Previous design?
I WORKED FOR A FREELANCE
GRAPHIC DESIGNER IN COLUMBIA,
SOUTH CAROLINA FOR SIX MONTHS
RIGHT AFTER GRADUATING COLLEGE
IN JUNE 1991. I CAME TO BOZEMAN
IN JANUARY 1992 AND STARTED MY
OWN BUSINESS. IT'S A GRIND TO
WORK FOR YOURSELF BUT WORTH
THE FREEDOM.

Where did you grow up ?
ON A RANCH ABOUT
30 MILES SOUTH
OF ENNIS, MONTANA!

115

JENAE NEESON
Clark Creative Group
Creative Director
Omaha, NE

JENAE NEESON

What have you learned from working at Clark Creative Group?

Getting a job with Clark Creative Group was a sling shot into the fast and furious world of advertising. Handling everything from ID packages, brochures, print ads, storyboards, billboards and so forth. You learn to juggle and switch design modes quickly when you have clients ranging from medical colleges to contemporary art museums to outdoor gear shops.

Advice for a designer?

Be sure to follow the three laws of design.

1. Work hard!
2. Play hard!
3. And respect type!

The Beautiful Waitress
Jo Harvey Allen

"THANKS LITTLE HONEY, WITH A TOUCH OF THE HAND AND SOME CHANGE"

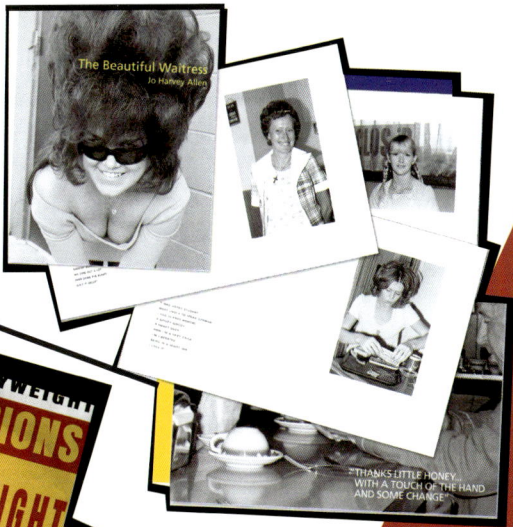

OMAHA'S OUTSTANDING HEAVYWEIGHT
BATTLE OF AD CHAMPIONS
★ A GRAND ASSAULT AT ARMS!! ★
★ MAIN EVENT ★
10-YEAR GRUDGE FIGHT
(YEAR ANNIVERSARY)
ACTION!!
THRILLS!!
IMPACT!!
★ THE BATTLE ALL OMAHA HAS BEEN WAITING FOR ★
THURSDAY, OCT. 17
BOUT STARTS AT 4 P.M.
CLARK CREATIVE GROUP
★★★ 10 ROUNDS — LIVE AND EXCLUSIVE!! ★★★
ROUND BY ROUND
★ DIRECT FROM JACKSON PLACE ARENA
CLARK CREATIVE GROUP — 514 SOUTH 13TH STREET OMAHA, NE — 345-5800

BY POPULAR DEMAND
★ THE CONTENDERS ★
FEARLESS FREDDY CLARK
Meaner than Hell MEL CLARK
Rabid ROX ABBOTT
MARK "Wilmashu" RYAN
MICHAEL mayhem MEEHAN
Left-Hook LISA NORTON
TRISHA "the Time Bomb" SCHMITZ
SCRAPPY SARA LITTLE
KEVIN "THE KRUSHER" REINER
LORI "The Police Powerhouse" KRENC
NASTY NAE NEESON
DEMOLITION DARYL ANDERSON
DEE-lusional WARREN

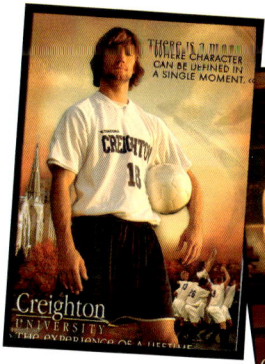

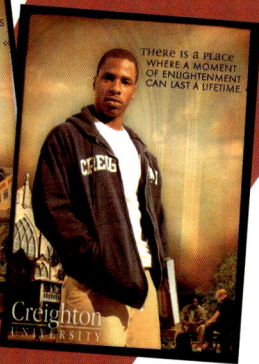

TAKE ON YOUR FAVORITE
★★★ CLARK CREATIVE GROUP ★★★
CONTENDER

THERE IS A PLACE WHERE CHARACTER CAN BE DEFINED IN A SINGLE MOMENT.
Creighton UNIVERSITY
THE EXPERIENCE OF A LIFETIME

THERE IS A PLACE WHERE EXPERIENCES CAN SHAPE A LIFELONG CAREER.
Creighton UNIVERSITY

THERE IS A PLACE WHERE A MOMENT OF ENLIGHTENMENT CAN LAST A LIFETIME.
Creighton UNIVERSITY

ERIK "OLE" NELSON

Owner/Artist
Media Station Design Works
Bozeman, MT

When did you begin working with metal?
I took many sculpture classes in addition to my graphic design classes. As a sophomore, I started working for Rijline Metal Art and helped them with hand torching metal as well as converting their hand torched images into machine-cut parts.

How long does each project take to complete?
On average, each sign takes around five weeks to finish.

What media do you use?
Mostly metal and glass, the most common are steel and neon. My current focus is on incorporating aluminum and moving forward with the antiquing process.

Where are you currently working?
My company is called Media Station Design Works. In October of 1995, I bought out Murphy's Signs and Graphics with a friend. We changed the name to Samolean and worked together until 2000 when I bought the company and changed it to Media Station Design Works.

How do you get projects?
Very little advertising is needed, most work is found by word of mouth. Most of my signs are local, but I have recently done some commissioned work for other artists.

Bull's Eye

FIRE DEPT. No. 9

NORTH STAR ENTERPR

the Nest
salon & spa

PLOnk
WINE

2ND BISTRO STREET

Floral Gallery

Gourmet Frank Sandwiches & Sou

BIG SKY

HTi
HOME TECHNOLOGY INTEGRATION

MAIN STREET
ARMY NAVY
SPORTS & OUTDOORS

Savory Olive

SOUP SHACK

Indulgence

SOMA

SOMA

What is Classic Ink?

We are a full service graphic design studio, compromised of four designers, all MSU graduates, and an administrative assistant.

Kietra Nelson
Classic Ink ▪ Bozeman, MT

What was the hardest part of getting your own design studio going?

Acquiring new clients. I fortunately had a job in furniture retail and design before I started Classic Ink, which gave me experience in sales and customer service. Meeting deadlines and doing great design work has helped the word travel fast.

What is your current job status?

I am the owner of Classic Ink. I do as much graphic design as I can. Unfortunately I end up doing more administrative work as we grow larger.

What do you find yourself designing mostly?

Logos, definitely. Although there is quite a bit of layout, including brochures, catalogs, posters, identity package, and package design.

Is being a Graphic Designer what you imagined it would be while you were in school?

Pretty close. There were several areas I had to learn on my own, and fast.

Where are you from?

Madison, Wisconsin

121

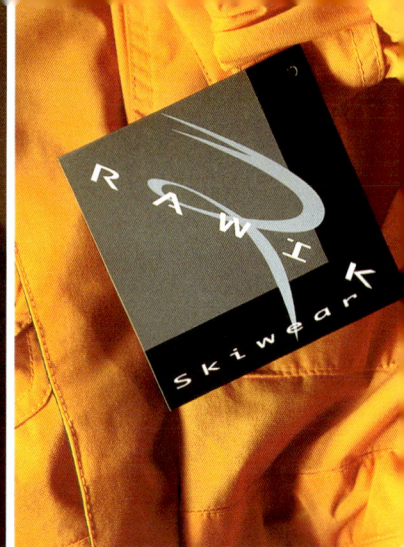

KURT PALMQUIST
Managing Partner
Creative Director
Ripple Marketing
Bozeman, MT

What advice do you have for graphic designers?

Even though this is an art related field, you still need to be a business professional. Also, you need to be a good communicator. Get to know the marketing side of the business (marketing research, strategic planning, etc). Your clients are going to want to know what they can do to reach their target audience and what motivates them to purchase. As a designer you have the tools to do just this, but you also need to know what the best plan is. We have to learn to be in a position to consult with them on the best approach, instead of just doing what they think they need.

What motivated you to become a designer?

I looked into the field a little more and found that it was something that really excited me. Back then I don't think I even realized what I was really getting into and how the field would grow to what it is today. There weren't very many people going into it at the time.

CAROL PATTERSON
Senior Designer
Life-Link International
Bozeman, MT

Do you have any words of wisdom for graduating seniors or any future designers?

Be flexible and fearless. After you graduate you will learn a lot about working in the real world of graphic design. You'll have great projects and fantastic clients. You'll also have difficult projects and equally tough clients. If you're smart, creative and flexible you can usually work out good solutions. Have a good sense about your strengths and style, but also be willing to teach yourself new things. The scope of what we do as graphic designers is growing at such a rapid pace that it seems like you always have to be ready to learn something new. The fact that the technology we use changes so rapidly makes it mandatory that we evolve as designers as well. If you embrace change and the opportunity to learn you'll probably be more successful.

Where do you get your inspiration?

I'm always looking at everything . . . whether it is the shape and play of light on a building, the motion and transparency of water, a discarded piece of trash, or the neon brightness of some tacky sign. I feel that as a designer you have to plug into the world around you and absorb as much as you can. You can find inspiration in almost anything.

What are your favorite types of projects?

I love working on packaging projects. The process of developing thoughtful, creative and yet practical packaging for three dimensional objects intrigues me. It's a puzzle that has to be solved on many levels. You're trying to come up with something functional and yet still engaging and appealing to the consumer. I also enjoy working on designs and patterns for textile applications. It's the type of project that falls outside of the normal realm of what I do on a daily basis.

shovels
Life-Link shovels are ideal for backcountry skiing and boarding, camping, building kickers, car emergencies and of course they are a great avalanche safety tool.

LIFE-LINK
backcountry travel

backpacks
Designed by skiers and snowboarders for skiers and snowboarders Life-Link packs perform - period.

LIFE-LINK
backcountry travel

slingblade
An ultra-light shovel and probe carrying system.

LIFE-LINK
backcountry travel

fresh
announcing croakies new tropical prints
for more information call 800.443.8620
or email croakies@croakies.com
Croakies

innovative
announcing croakies new tropical prints
for more information call 800.443.8620
or email croakies@croakies.com
Croakies

exciting
announcing croakies new tropical prints
for more information call 800.443.8620
or email croakies@croakies.com
Croakies

sublime
announcing croakies new tropical prints
for more information call 800.443.8620
or email croakies@croakies.com
Croakies

125

Julie Pfleger

Wild West Shirt Company
Bozeman, MT

What are some of your passions?
In my spare time I like to belly dance. I've been in the Middle Eastern dance troupe "The Caravan of Dreams" for 16 years. Wow! Am I that old already? I also do canine agility with my dog, Webley. I love to travel, eat good food and drink wine.

Why did you choose design as a career?
It was a practical way to find employment in the art field, and I enjoy the fusion of imagery with type.

Where does the majority of WWSC's clientele come from?
The majority of our clientele come from national parks throughout the United States. That is what we are best known for.

Do you design for national parks year-round?
WWSC designs two lines of shirts each year for the winter and summer seasons. We also do design for many local schools, local events, and ski resorts such as Vail and Tahoe.

What is the most satisfying aspect of your job?
Being able to see the fast results of my work from the start of the design, to the finished product on racks.

What advice would you give to an aspiring designer?
That's simple, be a good employee.

BOZEMAN ✿ MONTANA

©WWSC

Sweet Pea

FESTIVAL OF THE ARTS

• 2004 •

Yellowstone

SINCE 1872

QUALITY OUTDOOR GEAR

NATIONAL PARK

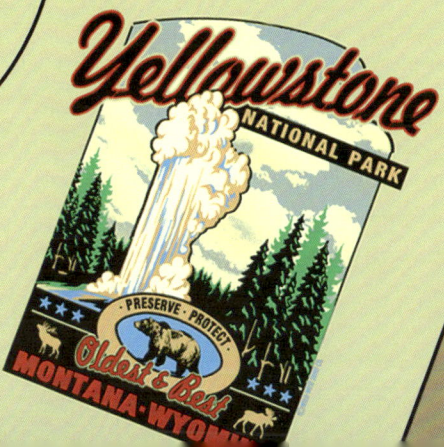

Yellowstone

NATIONAL PARK

PRESERVE · PROTECT

Oldest & Best

MONTANA · WYOMI

127

Chicago Social

CATHERINE **PILGRIM**

Associate Production Manager
Modern Luxury Magazines
Chicago, IL

Catherine, where did you grow up?
In the wonderful state of Indiana.

What advice would you give a designer?
Be resourceful. Meet as many people as possible in order to get a job, any job!
I ran into an MSU friend at Blockbuster in Chicago when I first moved here. We
had breakfast the next day and he suggested I call his old neighbor who got
me an internship at the company I now work for. Don't think you are above
a retail or a restaurant job. I worked in cosmetics for a year right after graduation and now I freelance as a make-up artist for MAC on the side.

What time of the year are you most productive?
Definitely in the beginning of the year, January to March, when it's absolutely
freezing in Chicago. But even then it's hard to stay inside, since I like to be as
busy as possible.

Where do you see yourself in five years?
Doing illustration or some other type of freelance work.

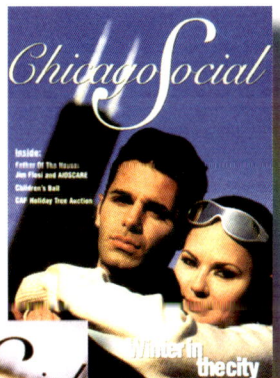

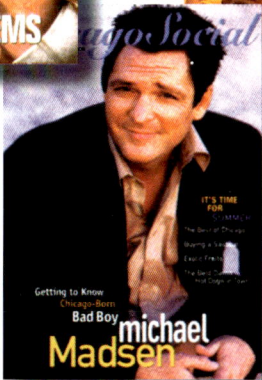

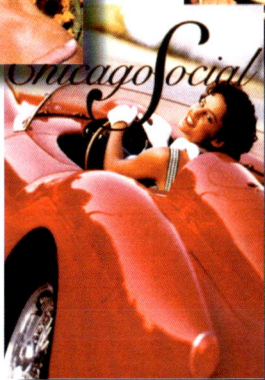

BRIDGET PRESTON

- Western Regional Graphic Designer
- WAC
- Seattle, WA

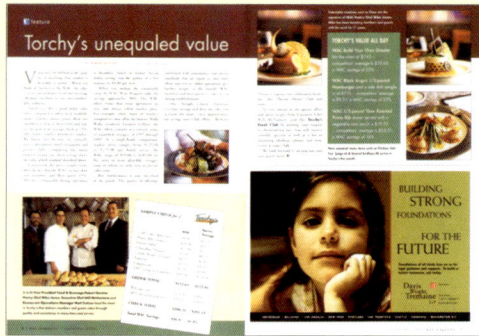

I have always had a need to deliver information, but my interest in graphic design was sparked while working on my high school newspaper. I had a knack for the Mac and could paste-up a dummy with frightening precision. I'll admit I was scared when I realized I would need to major in art to pursue a career in graphic design. With only one art class under my belt, I enrolled in Montana State University's graphic design program. I emerged four years later with a BA and a love of fine art.

My first paid gig was designing promotional materials for the Exit Gallery. The experience was a great asset when I relocated to Seattle in 1998. Effective Design Studio (EDS) hired me as a young designer. At EDS I worked on a wide variety of projects ranging from print collateral to large 3D installations.

In 2000 I snatched an opportunity to design a monthly magazine for the Washington Athletic Club (WAC). Over the years I gave the publication a more polished, professional look and I'm proud to say that advertisers took note. The magazine's revenue now outpaces its costs for the first time. In 2003 I was promoted to Senior Graphic Designer at WAC. Being part of an in-house marketing team has rounded out my skill set.

WASHINGTON ATHLETIC CLUB MAGAZINE

WAC

SEPTEMBER 2003

Torchy's Unequaled
in quality & value

wac.net

April

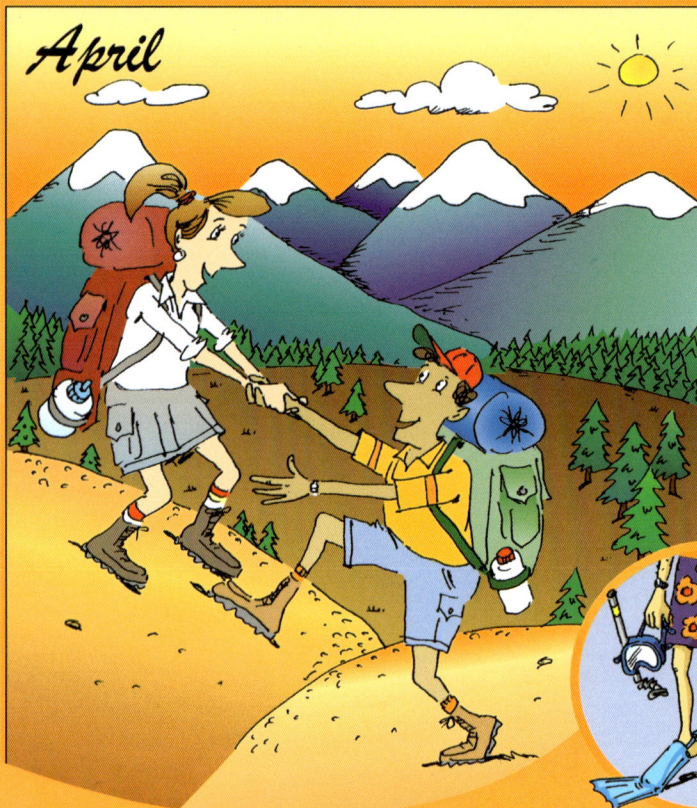

Put Some Spring *In Your Step*

Need motivation to get moving? Here are 5 ways to fit extra exercise into your weekly plans:

1. Create convenience. Choose an activity and time slot that fits smoothly into your schedule like first thing in the morning.

2. Make it enjoyable. Maybe you love swimming, the solitude of a morning walk or the music and company of an acrobics class.

3. Vary your activities. Variation prevents boredom and provides backup for weather or schedule changes.

4. Find an exercise partner. The energy and enthusiasm of a friend can help motivate you.

5. Set a 20-minute rule. Promise yourself that, even when you're tired or rushed, you'll do a light workout on your scheduled days rather than skip it completely.

As the warmer months approach, get ready to turn up the energy when you exercise.

2005

CANCER MONTH

Cancer Odds

Your risk of getting cancer depends on several factors – primarily age, lifestyle and family history. Fortunately, the body has natural defenses that rally to eliminate cancer-causing agents most of the time before damage occurs.

And since a third of all cancer is preventable, you can improve your odds against it:

• **Know** your risks.

• **Avoid** tobacco, alcohol and exposure to excess sunlight or hazardous chemicals.

• **Build** your defenses with diet and weight control.

• **See** your provider for regular cancer screenings.

RECORD Daily Exercise Time *here*

April Observances: STD Awareness Month (U.S.) • Foot Health Awareness Month (U.S.) • Dental Health Month (Canada)

SUNDAY	MONDAY	TUESDAY	WEDNESDAY	THURSDAY	FRIDAY	SATURDAY
MARCH 2005	MAY 2005		MORE INFO. Articles & Recipes www.investinyour health2005.com		1	2
3 Daylight Savings Time Begins	4	5	6	7	8	9
10	11	12	13	14	15	16
17	18	19	20	21	22	23
24 First Day of Passover	25	26	27	28	29	30 Last Day of Passover

MARCH 2005
S M T W T F S
        1 2 3 4 5
 6 7 8 9 10 11 12
13 14 15 16 17 18 19
20 21 22 23 24 25 26
27 28 29 30 31

MAY 2005
S M T W T F S
 1 2 3 4 5 6 7
 8 9 10 11 12 13 14
15 16 17 18 19 20 21
22 23 24 25 26 27 28
29 30 31

The Smart Woman's Guide to Health

The secret to looking and feeling your best at any age isn't a new hairdo or the latest diet fad. It's as simple as adopting good health habits now that can help you prevent disease, stay strong and enjoy life.

Personal Best.

To Prevent Osteoarthritis

Protect Your Joints

Osteoarthritis is a degenerative joint disease – but you don't have to be old to feel the pain. It's becoming more prevalent at earlier ages than in the past. Learn the facts about this common disability while you can still fight it.

Personal Best.

Balancing Act

The triple agenda – juggling job, self and everything else. How can you pursue meaningful work, care for yourself, and be there for others at the same time? It's easier once you learn to make smart choices.

Personal Best.

Heather M. Preston
Art Director • Scott Publishing Inc. • Seattle, WA

WHAT IS IT LIKE COMING FROM A FAMILY OF GRAPHIC DESIGNERS?

I think it is great coming from a creative family. I have two uncles who were designers and one who was an art teacher, so it runs in the family. I am the oldest of four children and three of us are designers. We are all three years apart so there really was no competition. Since school, my younger sister Bridget has worked with me on projects and we come up with great solutions by working together. As for my brother, he is three years younger than Bridget and very new to the design workplace, so we definitely don't have competition, but he thinks of me as a mentor and phone tech support in a jam.

WHERE ARE YOU WORKING NOW?

I art direct wellness material for Scott Publishing Inc. in Edmonds, Washington. I design the yearly calendars, monthly newsletters, brochures, marketing material, and other custom projects. I also oversee two designers and two editors. I schedule printers, quote projects and divide the workload, as well as select photos and coordinate project flow. I am a member of the management team that selects marketing strategy, corporate direction and new product development. The president/editor in chief, myself and the marketing manager select marketing slogans, calendar topics design, and budget the departments. Since I have been with this company we have doubled in size and have increased our quantity of calendars sold yearly from 120,000 to 500,000. We have designed custom products for the Veterans of the United States, Welmark Blue Cross Blue Shield, Washington Mutual, Principal Financial and Safeco Bank.

WHO ARE SOME OF YOUR PREVIOUS DESIGN EMPLOYERS?

I worked at Bay Printing in Oak Harbor, Washington for one and a half years and then at Pacific Copy and Printing in Everett, Washington for one year. I worked mostly in the output and design departments where I learned a lot about output and what presses and ink can be made to do.

What are your favorite projects ?

I enjoy any project with a deadline in the distant future, but I especially like pen & ink cartoony illustrations. They seem to come most naturally from thumbnail to final execution.

Favorite font?

Copperplate 33BC

What are you working on now?

I am currently working at Wild West Shirt Works in Seattle, Washington. I'm mostly involved with designing and illustrating t-shirt art, logo creation and flash-based web design.

What is the most enjoyable part of your job?

Early on in a project when I get to take my time doing research and imagining what it will look like. But probably the best part is the relief of getting final approval on a project and liking the results. Everything in between has a very high-stress potential.

Who are your previous employers?

Fuze Technologies, LJB Productions, and Strand Union Graphics at MSU.

134

Carlos Radillo

Graphic Designer • Wild West Shirt Works • Seattle, WA

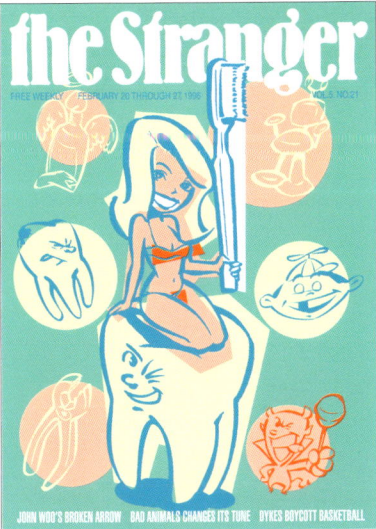

ROBERT RATH

What is your best advice for a young graphic designer?
Work hard, play fair, and marry someone with money.

When working on your own personal artwork, what does it consist of?
Lots of anguish and severe bouts of depression. I've realized there's a reason I'm a designer and an illustrator instead of a "fine artist." I like having assignments and deadlines. I enjoy working with other people to find the best way to communicate their needs. When I try to do something strictly for myself, I am a horrible perfectionist; all my ideas are dumb, I'm never happy with how anything looks, and I never finish anything.

136

Goosebumps

ROBERT RATH
Illustrator/Designer
Self Employed
Bozeman MT

Where do you look for inspiration?

Usually the calendar. Deadlines come up so fast that there really isn't time for listening to the Muse. I'm finding lately that I look less to art for inspiration, and more to the artists themselves. I see how hard other designers, writers, illustrators, architects, astronauts, doctors, teachers, musicians and filmmakers are working and that makes me want to work harder and do better projects.

What medium do you most commonly use when completing your illustrations?

I draw everything by hand, usually with ink, but more and more with just pencil and then scan it into Photoshop and do any coloring with that. Lots of times I'll scan other texture elements, paint splatters, brushy things that I layer into the image just to give it that extra hand-made look.

Who are you working for and what is your favorite project?

I've been a freelance book designer and illustrator for almost 10 years now. I've had a lot of fun working on some very entertaining books, but as a geek, one of my favorite projects was working on Star Wars stuff and getting "Top Secret" reference packages from Lucasfilm before the last batch of movies came out.

MONTANA
STATE UNIVERSITY
B O Z E M A N

EST. 1897
LEHRKIND
MANSION
BED AND BREAKFAST

WHOA!

137

annie regnier

Columbia Sportswear Company
Portland, OR

What's your favorite spot in Portland?

The paper store . . . I'm obsessed with paper.

Why did you choose MSU?

I couldn't wait to get out of Montana after high school. I attended school in Wisconsin, Washington and Spain until I ended up back in Montana. I cannot tell you how much I draw on my education from MSU. I have never had an art director be as discriminating, but inspiring, as Anne Garner.

I remember my first interview. The interviewer told me, they had 75 applicants for this job. They chose ten people to interview and five of them were from MSU.

Any advice for a graduating senior?

First of all, diversify your portfolio. Take on additional projects that you can show in your portfolio. Secondly, get to know printers. Printers hold a wealth of knowledge that they are willing to impart if you take interest. Go down to a local print shop and watch a four-color job on press and have them explain what the process is.

Do you have some words of wisdom?

No matter how bad a job is, don't burn any bridges and always be gracious. At the same time, don't let yourself get walked over.

TECH SUPPORT

HOLLYWOOD VIDEO

ModerN ❋ BOUQUET

radish
DESIGNS

HOOD RIVER, OREGON
ph 541.380.0528

bmk

portland, oregon

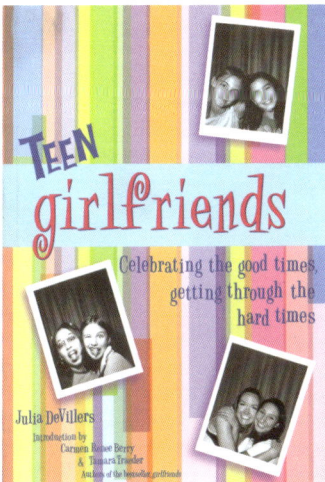

February

TEEN
girlfriends

Celebrating the good times,
getting through the
hard times

Julia DeVillers

Introduction by
Carmen Renee Berry
& Tamara Traeder
Authors of the bestseller girlfriends

love

139

SUE SAVAGE
Divisional Vice President
E-commerce Creative
Coldwater Creek
Sandpoint, ID

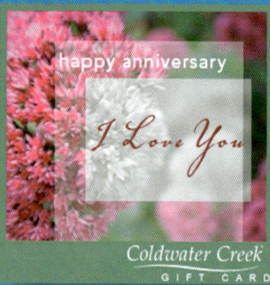

Did you have an internship before graduating?
No I didn't, but I did work at the SUB Graphics shop for two years while in school. The first year I was a designer. The second year I was the manager. I feel the largest benefit from this job was client contact.

How long did it take until you found a design job?
It took less than a year.

As department head, what do you look for when hiring a designer?
Utmost professionalism!

Do you like art directing more than designing?
It is hard to say because they require a significantly different focus. I love working with others, developing the vision and the fast pace of the job.

Did you have any design jobs prior to this one?
I was an art director for Wendt Advertising in Great Falls, MT prior to my current job. During my eight years at Coldwater Creek, I have been a graphic designer focused on the catalog, art director for photo shoots ranging from product to national ad campaigns, lead designer/information architect for the internet, design manager, and design director for the internet. I have had my current role for roughly two years.

Karen Schmidt
Graphic Designer
K-Graphics
Bozeman, MT

What are your main duties as the art director for Big Sky Journal?
Imposition and layout of each issue. Image selection, assigning photographers to stories. Working with the editor, publisher, ad designer and printer to coordinate production and print schedules. Concept-layout for a bimonthly postcard and the annual media kit.

When did you become art director?
May 2003

What design work did you do immediately out of school?
A lot of print collateral for Big Sky Resort - brochures, billboards, newspaper and magazine ads, along with logos and brochures for new businesses.

Who were your previous design employers?
I have always been a freelancer. Here's a partial list of clients: Big Sky Journal, H.S. Trask and Co., Leaf and Bean, Bridger Bowl, Big Sky Resort, Arts Market, the National Endowment for the Arts, Museum of the Rockies, Greater Yellowstone Coalition, and more.

Where did you grow up?
North Shore of Boston - Danvers, Massachusetts!

Any last thoughts on design?
Graphic design is a treasure hunt and a puzzle.

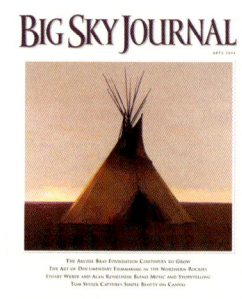

BIG SKY JOURNAL

FALL 2004

ELIZABETH DAVEY LOCHRIE: ARMED WITH GUN AND SKETCHPAD

JENNIFER OLSSON SPINS A WOOLLY TALE

CHRIS DOMBROWSKI TELLS OF BOLD PHEASANT AND ELUSIVE WHITEFISH

JOHN HOLT CAPTURES A PERFECT FALL DAY

Where is the snow-board aesthetic headed in the next few years?

The aesthetics will be going backward and forward. Big styles I see for the coming 2005/2006 season are 1980's graphics, notebook doodle-type illustrations, and an emphasis on color.

What are your cultural and social influences?

Seattle's industrial areas, foreign food markets, and street art have influenced me in the last few years. I have developed a great appreciation for Mexican street art, urban graffiti, architectural and engineering elements in modern and old industry, Asian food packaging, and Japanese printing techniques.

How did you get involved in the snowboard industry?

I began work at EXPN.com in Los Angeles, and then an opening with RIDE snowboards in Seattle got me into the industry I'm in now.

CHRISTIAN SCHULTZ

Web and Graphic Designer
Northwave/Piva Co.
Seattle, WA

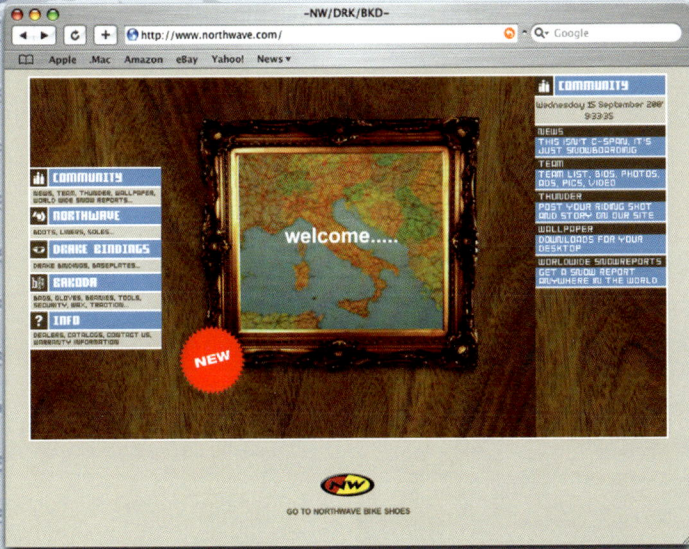

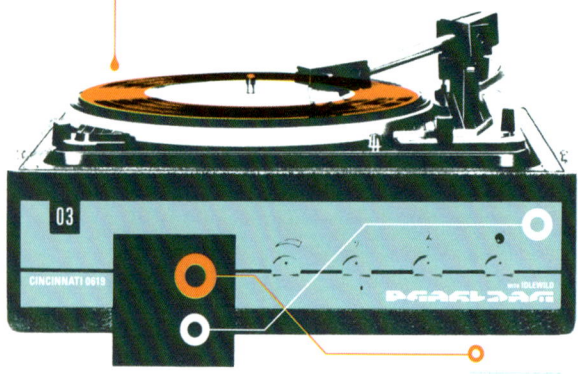

What is it like designing in Seattle?

Seattle has been good to me. Being part of a city has it's ups and downs. I generally avoid anything associated with a metropolitan area. It is the underbelly of Seattle that I take full advantage of. Obscure bookstores, magazines, food, easy access to fresh air and the outdoors, water . . . these all mold my Seattle experience and in turn affect the way I design. There are a few people I really respect in the Seattle design community, but on the whole I do my own thing.

What sort of advice could you offer someone entering the design world?

Be creative!!! It ain't about print, web, brochures, logos, posters. It's about using what you learned in school to survive. Figure out what you want to do, although it may take awhile, and then do your best to accomplish it, knowing you've got to roll with the punches.

coby schultz

Ames Bros. Owner / Designer Seattle, WA

How has owning your own business improved your life?

By the time I finished my first year of design out of college, I knew that I couldn't work for somebody else, so to me it's not about how it improved my life, but it's how my life is. Whether I'm designing or something else, I'll probably always work for myself. Overall, I'd say it's improved my life and it's allowed me to do what I want to do and support my family. Not too bad.

PEARL JAM
with Buzzcocks
WASHINGTON DC · JULY 5 2003

A M E S

PEARL JAM

Ames is a full-service agency located in the heart of the Pacific Northwest known for their high level of illustration and keen eye for design. With extensive experience in the snowboard and music industry, this two man shop has emerged as a proven authority on youth culture branding. Ames has had a great deal of success connecting companies and their products to the elusive youth audience.

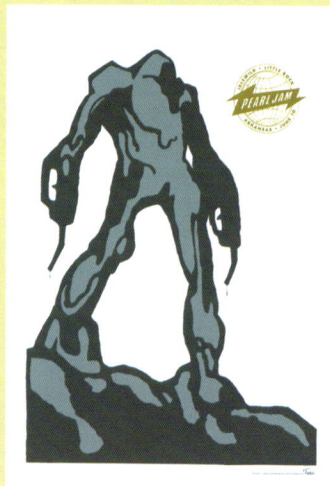

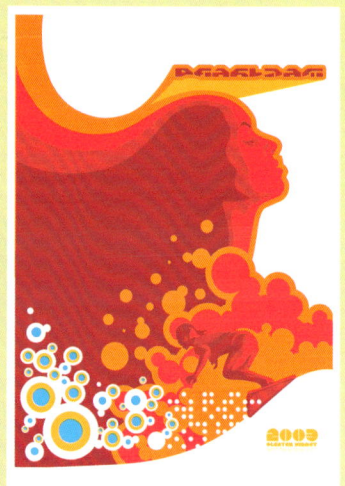

This shows in their history, partnering with snowboard companies like K2 and Ride, creating cutting-edge graphics each and every season. Ames has also been progressive in their approach to creating the visual identity of rock bands through unique and award-winning custom CD packaging and merchandise, most notably creating up to 100 limited editions event posters in a given year for the indie music scene, as well as for rock giants like Pearl Jam, Phish, John Mayer and Sting.

This progressive approach has given them an insider's point of view, that has been successfully applied to branding and marketing for much bigger fish such as MTV, Nike, Nissan, Honda, AOL, Got Milk?, Absolut and Virgin - among others.

coby schultz

A
M
E
S

LAND. SEA. AIR. BY ANY MEANS NECESSARY.

NEW YORK

SEATTLE

LONDON

TOKYO

149

JENNIFER SIMON-BECKER
Product Designer
Big Sky Carvers
Manhattan, MT

Q>> What have been the top three design influences of your design career?

A>> For me, inspiration is everywhere and I never know when I will see something that will

make a spark. Sometimes it's my family, nature, or sometimes something I see in

a store or on TV. I love packaging design from the 1900's to the 1960's. If I have to

pick three, let's just say my first, second, and third professional design jobs. With each

job I have gained so much experience and have been challenged with figuring out

how to get something done. In some cases ignorance is bliss, because nothing seems

impossible if you've never tried it before. Somehow you just make it work.

Q>> What are your obligations as a product designer?

A>> My focus is on creating new products for current and new customers, special accounts,

and new business. A recent highlight has been a trip to Asia where I visited

Hong Kong, China, and Taiwan to tour factories and meet our Asian partners in person to discuss current projects. As a developer, I am challenged with creating 50 100 or more new products about every six months. It is a constant cycle of concepts, prototypes, and following through with packaging.

Q>> What is your mission in design?

A>> Above all, do my best, always try to improve, and inspire others to do their best. Be self-motivating, and maintain a strong work ethic. Enjoy the work, have fun, and be open to new ideas and creativity.

Richard A. Smith, President
Daniel P. Smith, Vice President
Double Entendre, Inc.
Seattle, WA

Any advice?
Never give up! Follow your passion! (Daniel)
Create an image that will help you stand
out and be memorable. (Richard)
**If you were not a designer,
what would you be doing?**
Movie making (D)
Event planning (R)
Previous design employers?
Ghost Fighters, Cornish College of the Arts (D)
TRA Architects, Tim Girvin Design,
Microsoft Corp. (R)
Where are you working now?
On sabbatical in Maui, HI via the internet. (D)
1300 SW Webster St., Seattle, WA (R)
What aspect of design most interests you?
Solving the client's problem. (D)
Conceptual - coming up with ideas. (R)
Town/state where you grew up?
Polson, Montana! (D)
Polson, Montana! (R)
What is your favorite font?
Futura! (D)
Futura! (R)
Company?
Double Entendre, Inc. (D)
Double Entendre, Inc. (R)
Job Title?
President (D)
Vice President - Treasurer (R)
What is your favorite color?
Jasper Green! (D)
Celadon Green! (R)

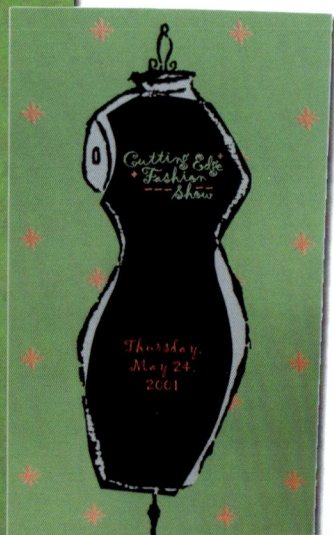

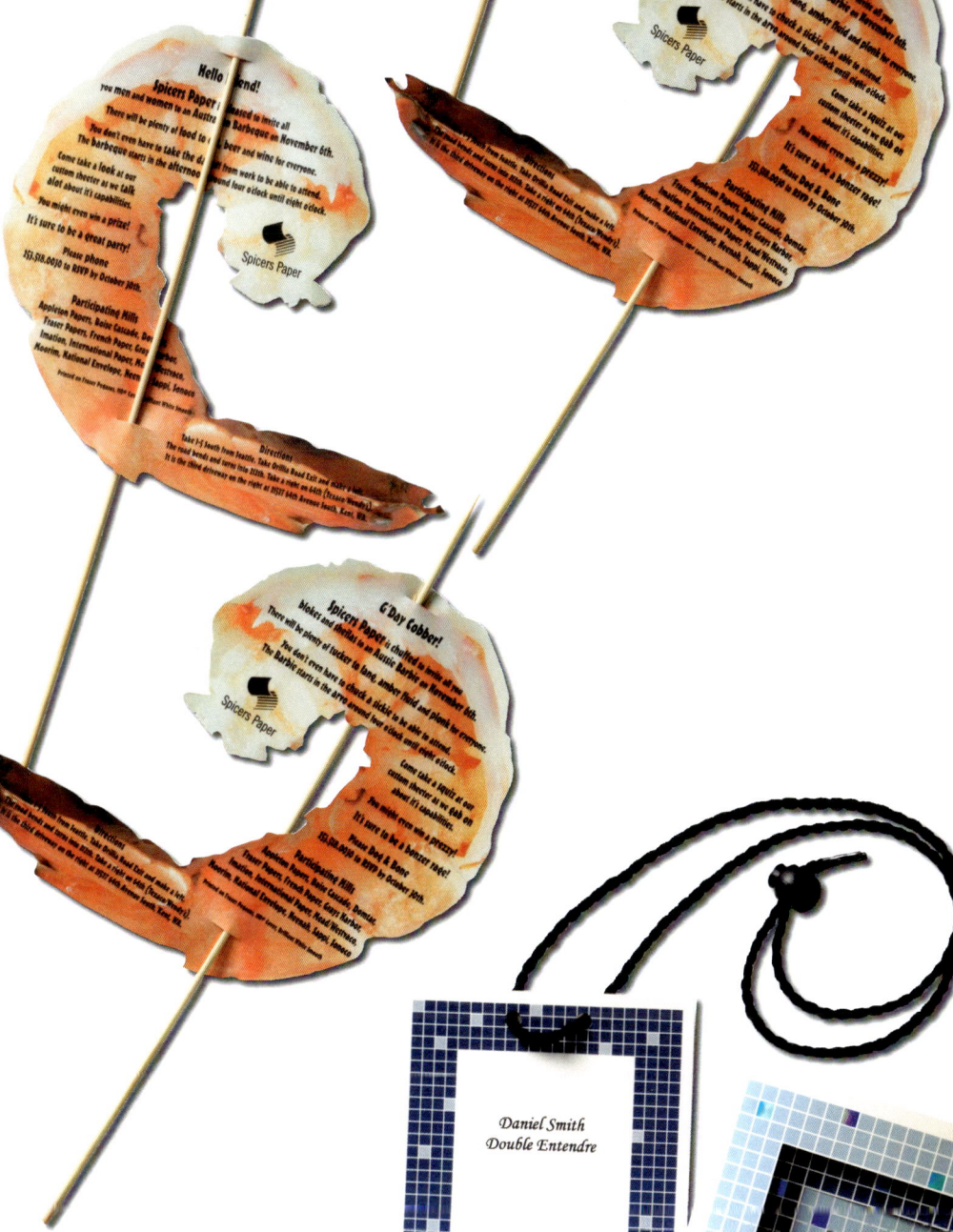

Hello Friend!

Spicers Paper is pleased to invite all you men and women to an Australian Barbeque on November 6th.

There will be plenty of food to eat. You don't even have to take the day off. The barbeque starts in the afternoon... beer and wine for everyone.

Come take a look at our custom shelter as we talk alot about it's capabilities.

You might even win a prize! It's sure to be a great party!

Please phone 253.518.0030 to RSVP by October 30th.

Participating Mills
Appleton Papers, Boise Cascade, Domtar, Fraser Papers, French Paper, Gray, Imation, International Paper, Mead Westvaco, Neenah, National Envelope, Nevamar, Sappi, Sonoco

Directions
Take I-5 south from Seattle. Take Orillia Road Exit and make a left. The road bends and turns into 515th. Take a right on 64th (Fraser Woods). It is the third driveway on the right at 8521 64th Avenue South, Kent, WA.

Spicers Paper

G'Day Cobber!

Spicers Paper is chuffed to invite all blokes and sheilas to an Aussie Barbie on November 6th.

There will be plenty of tucker to tuck in. You don't even have to take a sickie to be able to attend. The Barbie starts in the arvo around four o'clock until eight o'clock.

Come take a squiz at our custom shelter as we yack on about it's capabilities.

You might even win a prezzy!

It's sure to be a bonzer race!

Please Dial & Bone 253.518.0030 to RSVP by October 30th.

Participating Mills
Appleton Papers, Boise Cascade, Domtar, Fraser Papers, French Paper, Gray, Imation, International Paper, Mead Westvaco, Neenah, National Envelope, Nevamar, Sappi, Sonoco

Directions
Take I-5 south from Seattle. Take Orillia Road Exit and make a left. The road bends and turns into 515th. Take a right on 64th (Fraser Woods). It is the third driveway on the right at 8521 64th Avenue South, Kent, WA.

Spicers Paper

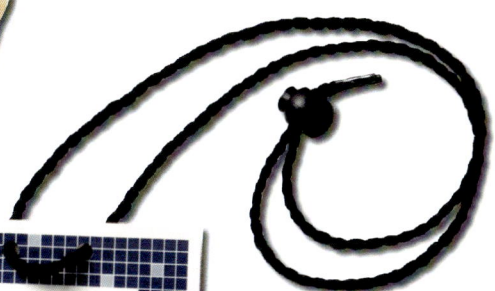

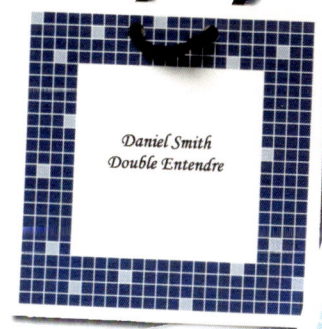

Daniel Smith
Double Entendre

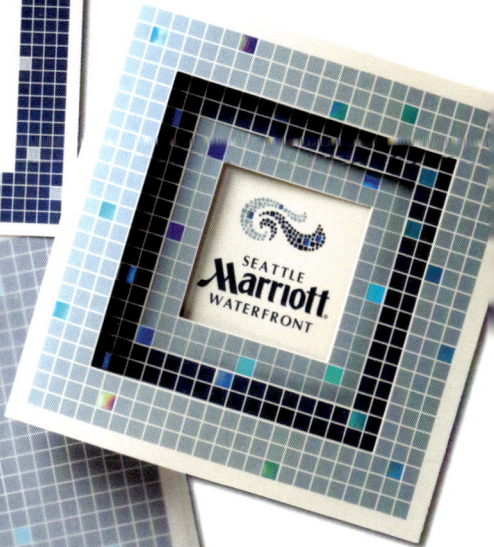

SEATTLE
Marriott
WATERFRONT

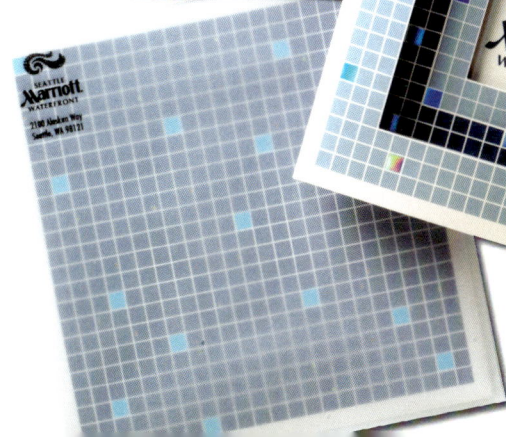

SEATTLE
Marriott
WATERFRONT
7100 Alaskan Way
Seattle, WA 98121

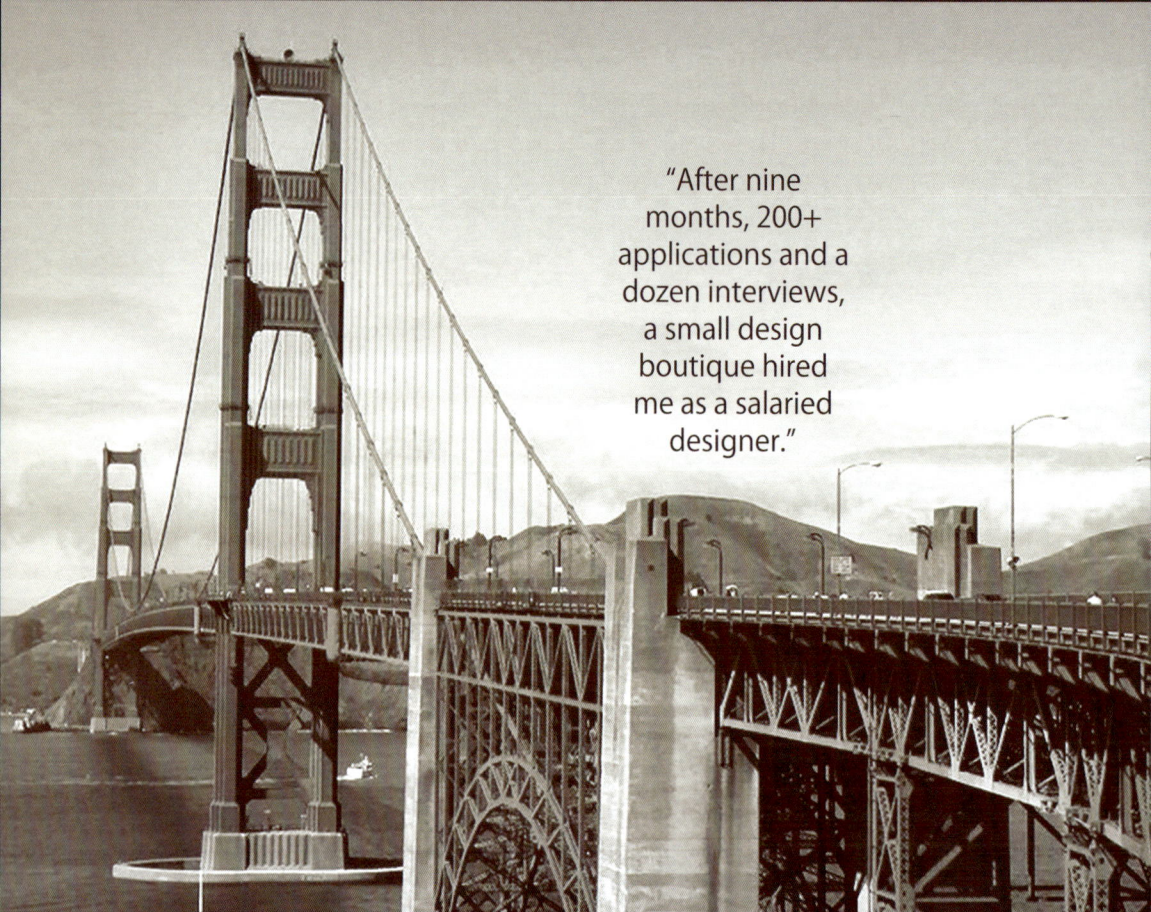

"After nine months, 200+ applications and a dozen interviews, a small design boutique hired me as a salaried designer."

Tell us about your life in Bozeman!

I arrived in Montana on the coattails of my future wife, Monica. To supplement my financial aid while attending classes, I started a production company with my friend. We brought many alternative bands to town. After graduating and relocating to San Francisco, the job search began.

What about your move to San Francisco!

After nine months, 200+ applications and a dozen interviews, a small design boutique hired me as a salaried designer. Seven years later, I'm still there. I'm currently living in Oakland with my wife and two kids and playing in the Amish punk band - Nuclear Barn!

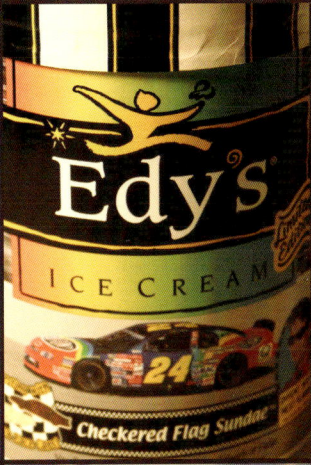

Amy Sowers
Graphic Designer
Wantulok Design
Bozeman, MT

What do you like to do in your spare time?
I like hot rods and I like to sew. I guess those
don't really go together do they?

**What is the most important thing you learned
during your job application process after college?**
Getting your foot in the door anywhere is important.
Doing the production work as a means to learn the
ropes is sometimes a drag, but totally worth it.

What were your inspirations in college?
Anything ... everything ... sometimes nothing.

amy sowers

HE BOSS
Hands up, chin down, keep moving forward!
BOZEMAN
BOXING ★ CLUB
EQUIPMENT
YOUR OPPONENT IS TRAINING HARDER THAN YOU ARE!!
the sweet science
BOXERS
KATE
THE SNAKE
ROSS
TAMMY
THE BONE
CRUSHER
TRIBBET
NOAH
THE FIGHTING
DUTCHMAN
ten BROEK

BOZEMAN
BOXING ★ CLUB
US Amateur Boxing

**IF YOU WERE NOT A DESIGNER,
WHAT WOULD YOU WANT TO BE DOING?**

Playing professional soccer!

WHAT IS SOME ADVICE FOR THOSE ENTERING THE FIELD?

Balance confidence with fear of failure.
Invest in a good chair.

WHAT IS YOUR FAVORITE COLOR?

Cashmere - It is a Martha Stewart wall paint . . .
the lady knows her colors.

WHAT IS YOUR FAVORITE FONT?

DIN Shriften

TOWN/STATE WHERE YOU GREW UP?

Lake Tahoe, Nevada

WHERE ARE YOU WORKING NOW?

Bozeman, Montana

COMPANY?

Future Farm

PREVIOUS DESIGN EMPLOYERS:

Earthtalk Studios and Strategix ID

WHAT ASPECT OF DESIGN MOST INTERESTS YOU?

Interactive design!

WHAT IS YOUR JOB TITLE?

Owner, Project Manager
Marketing & Sales
Lead Programmer
Lead Designer and Janitor!

INFO | 360° VIEW

Cheyenne Troupe

Cheyenne Rivers Studio
Graphic Designer | Photographer
Florence, MT

You have been busy since MSU, tell us what you've been up to.

Graphic design and the art of photography have been in my life now for the past 14 years. I am very thankful for these skills and for the wonderful professors and many creative directors along the way that have shown me how to create beautiful typography and creative design. I was fortunate enough to have worked in a nationally known design firm in Boise for about six years, five of which were spent telecommuting for this firm from Montana. Recently, I have begun freelancing however, so I could encompass working more with clients and printers locally. I welcome you to visit my former firm's site at www.foerstel.com.

Within the past five years, photography has taken a stronger hold on me in addition to the graphic design. I am thankful for the Rocky Mountain School of Photography and its staff here in Missoula, they have helped me fine tune my direction into black and white pregnancy photography and children's portraits, too.

Graphic design, as well as photography, are worlds open to possibility. To have this skill is wonderful and the doors for creativity are endless. These skills provide the opportunity for a balanced life of work and family, as I am able to work at home and still coordinate raising my children. I am currently working on a couple of books and a calendar that are my aspirations for future publication. Hats off to MSU. Thank you for all that you offer!

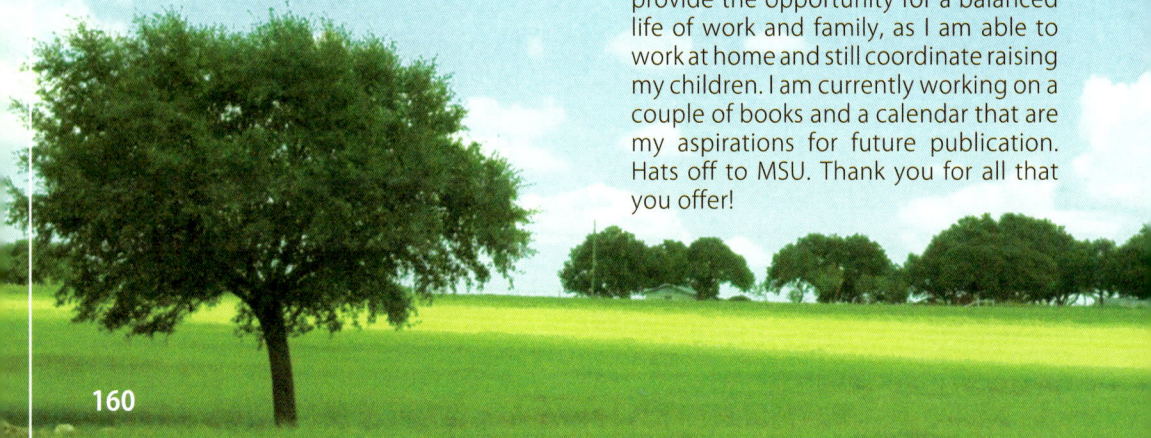

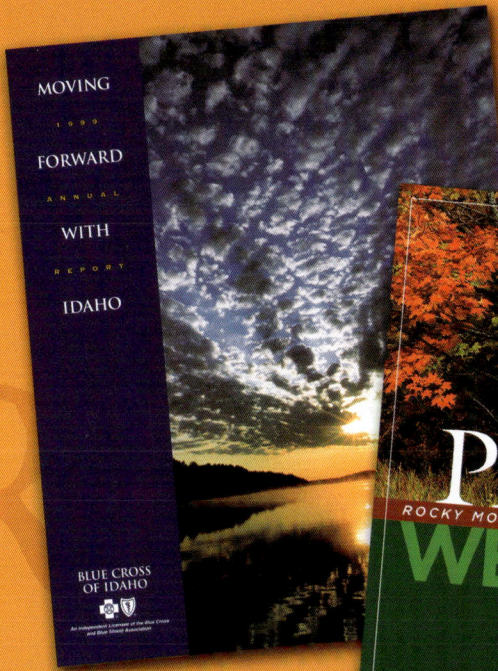

MOVING

1999

FORWARD

ANNUAL

WITH

REPORT

IDAHO

BLUE CROSS
OF IDAHO

An Independent Licensee of the Blue Cross
and Blue Shield Association

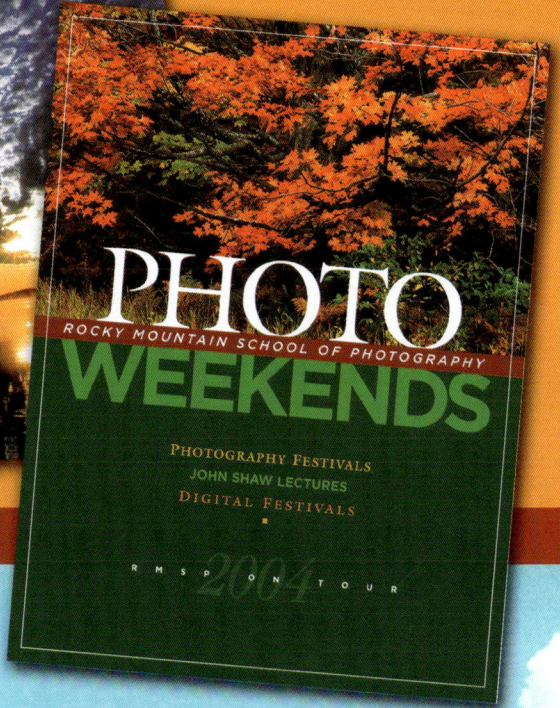

PHOTO
ROCKY MOUNTAIN SCHOOL OF PHOTOGRAPHY
WEEKENDS

PHOTOGRAPHY FESTIVALS
JOHN SHAW LECTURES
DIGITAL FESTIVALS

R M S P   O N   T O U R
2004

And this place OF REST WILL BE GLORIOUS.
ISAIAH 11:10

Rest

Rest was one of God's first and best rules. But in today's breathless pace of life and ministry, it's easy to lose sight of the fact that we are most centered on God... most satisfied by God most like God when our bodies and spirits are resting in Him.

"I HAVE BEEN SO BLESSED IN MY STAY HERE.
GOD DOESN'T NEED A LONG TIME TO REFRESH AND RENEW."

Burnt Fork Ranch is a place to disconnect from the demands of calendars and clocks, and reconnect with what matters most — the touch of your spouse, the voice of your Creator, the wonder of your place in the grandeur of His creation.

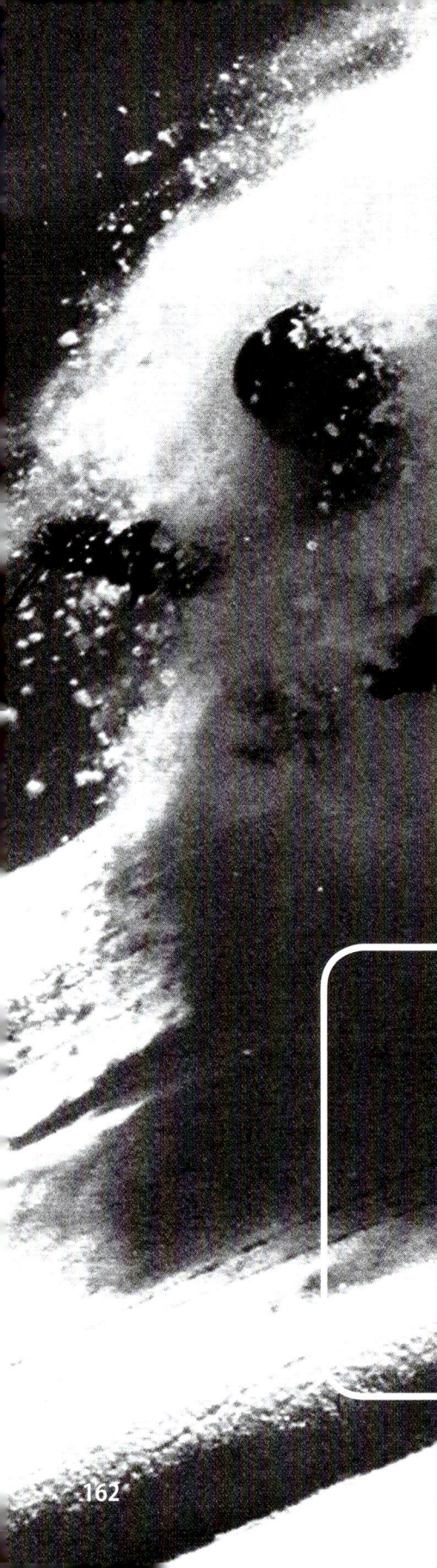

What was your favorite part about the School of Art at MSU?
In retrospect, it was the relationships with the instructors: Anne, Stephanie, Harvey, Robert, Rich and Clarice.

Where do you get inspiration?
I can be inspired by any environment I am in. German and soft modern Italian architecture and design interests me. I also love the work of Tuk and Finn VaughanKraska, Frida Kahlo, Raymond Meeks, Molly Merica, Robert Rath, Suzanne Truman and perhaps the current featured artist in Communication Arts magazine.

Why did you choose to stay in the Bozeman area?
It's beautiful and I can make a living doing a job I love.

Where is your hometown?
Spokane, WA and Talkeetna, AK.

Have you had any previous design employers?
Morrison Creative and Life-Link.

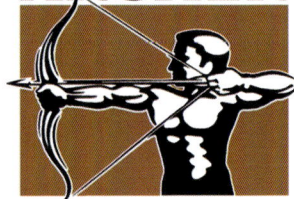

ARCHER

art + soul

IXTLA VAUGHAN
Owner/Graphic Designer
I Design
Bozeman, MT

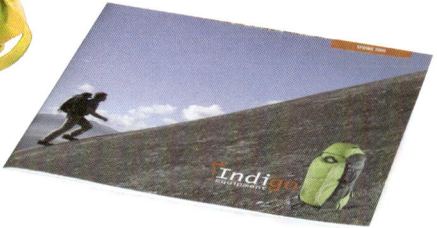

Is there an area in the arts that you think you could improve on?
I think film would be exciting, but I would probably make it more of a hobby.
I have already started with movies of my daughter and wife, working on my IMac at home.

Who have you worked for in the past?
Nike was my first real gig out of school. I also did a quick stint at a newspaper just to pay the bills!

What part of design do you like most?
I think the start is always exciting. I, also like sketching and brainstorming with the team I'm working with. No idea is a bad idea, and there are no wrong answers.

LIFETIME GUARANTEE

EXTRA BIG

Matt Wellman
Senior Graphic Designer
NIKE Portland, OR

ACG **SPRING 04**
It's a whole new world.

CONSUMER   TECHNOLOGY   BAGS   IN STORE

HOME   CONSUMER   TECHNOLOGY   BAGS   IN STORE   REPLAY INTRO
NIKEACG.COM

HANG **TAGS**

PHOTO**GRAPHY**

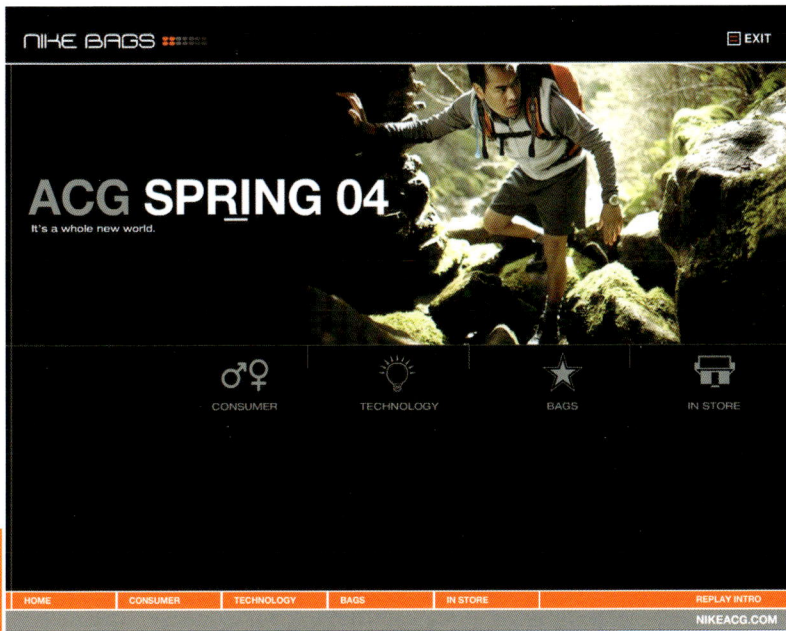

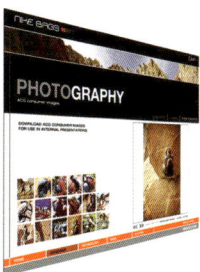

Where did you grow up?
Wasilla, Alaska - if you spell it backwards
it is "ALLISAW"... it's a very small town!

Who inspires or drives you most?
I get inspiration from everywhere!
Magazines are wonderful, the web is also a
great tool, but I think it's always important
to get out and see what's going on in the
world first hand; travel!

How long have you worked for Nike?
I freelanced for Nike for nine months
before I was brought on full time.
I think I have been here for about eight
years … it goes by fast!

165

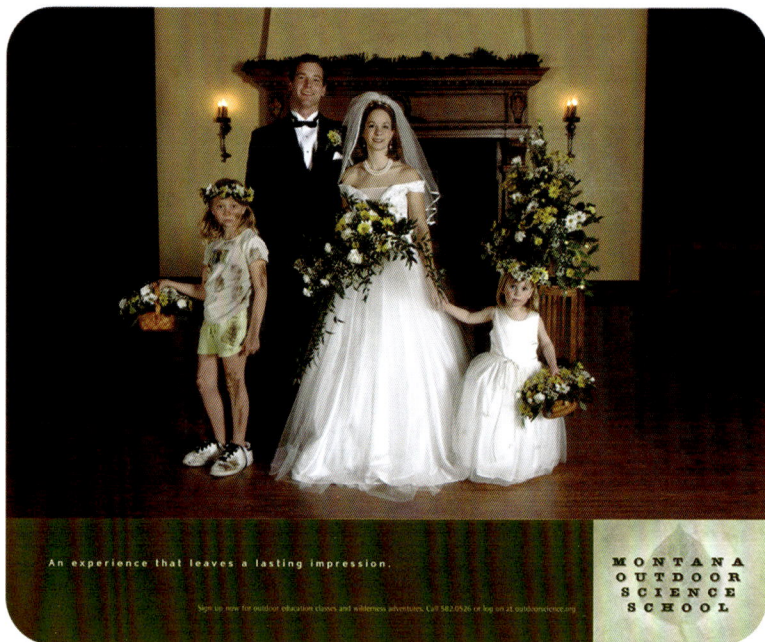

An experience that leaves a lasting impression.

Sign up now for outdoor education classes and wilderness adventures. Call 582.0526 or log on at outdoorscience.org

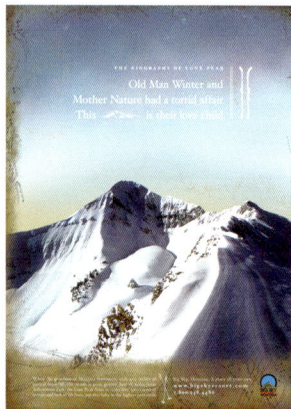

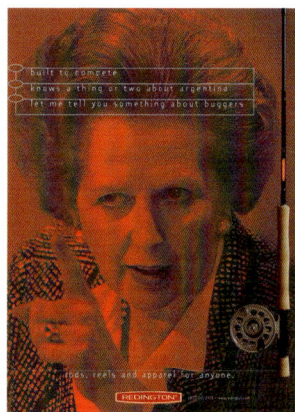

MONTANA OUTDOOR SCIENCE SCHOOL

Jamie Willett-Hurd
Partner / Creative Director
Mercury Advertising
Bozeman, MT

WHAT HAVE YOU BEEN UP TO SINCE MSU? I have been really committed to staying in Montana and doing great advertising for businesses in our state and region. I started doing work for my family's business - Showdown Ski Area and now I run a full service ad agency of fifteen people producing work in the areas of print, outdoor, television, radio, web and collateral design.

WHAT GOT YOU INTERESTED IN GRAPHIC DESIGN? Architecture and punk rock.

WHAT ARE SOME OF THE REWARDS OF BEING A DESIGNER? I believe that individuals, art, and social forces move markets and motivate consumers. Creating messages that attract consumers to our clients' brands is fun and rewarding.

WHAT ADVICE DO YOU HAVE FOR FUTURE GRAPHIC DESIGNERS? Know your client, know their goals, and give them something meaningful and integrated.

WHAT IS YOUR FAVORITE PROJECT THAT YOU HAVE WORKED ON? I like all projects that take risks. The bigger the risk, the bigger the potential reward.

IF ANYWHERE, WHERE WOULD YOU LIKE TO LIVE? Montana is where I choose to live. Traveling inspires me, but Montana gives me the freedom I need to create.

MERCURY
ADVERTISING

JEFF WILLIAMS
Designer
Tower Records
San Francisco, CA

m s

What are your favorite bands?

I like DJ Krush, Goapele and any of the classic jazz singers like Louis Armstrong and Tony Bennett.

What is the best part of being a designer?

Since most of the work I do is in advertising, I really like the challenge of trying to create an ad that makes people stop and smile, laugh or have any kind of emotional reaction. Of course the main purpose is to sell a product, but it is also nice to brighten someone's day.

Do you have enough time to ski, snowboard or vacation?

I am a terrible workaholic, so most of my evenings and weekends are spent working on design and illustration projects. But I do love spending time in San Francisco. It is an amazing city.

Would you rather own a design company or work for someone?

I like working for someone else. There are still a lot of small details I need to learn concerning typography and layout before I would be experienced enough to be a good art director.

Inspirations, mottoes or quotes to live by?

Listen to everyone's opinion, keep it simple, plan and measure everything, respect typography, work hard and remember how lucky you are.

Do you have many freelance projects?

I work full-time for a large company and I also do freelance work in the evenings and on the weekends.

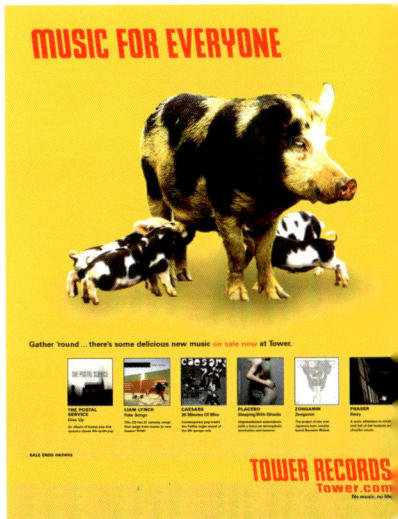

169

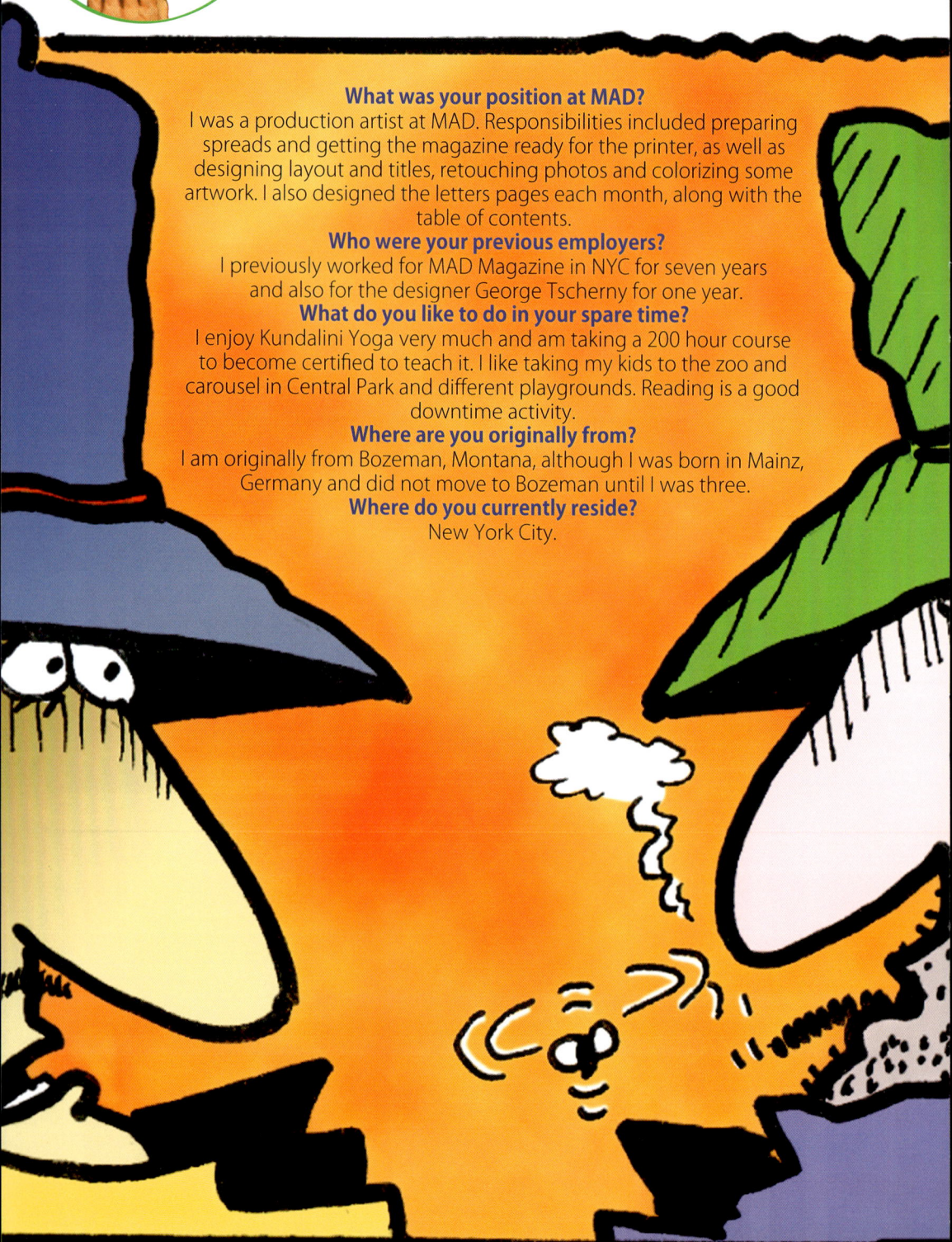

MarlaWyche
MAD Magazine, NYC

What was your position at MAD?
I was a production artist at MAD. Responsibilities included preparing spreads and getting the magazine ready for the printer, as well as designing layout and titles, retouching photos and colorizing some artwork. I also designed the letters pages each month, along with the table of contents.

Who were your previous employers?
I previously worked for MAD Magazine in NYC for seven years and also for the designer George Tscherny for one year.

What do you like to do in your spare time?
I enjoy Kundalini Yoga very much and am taking a 200 hour course to become certified to teach it. I like taking my kids to the zoo and carousel in Central Park and different playgrounds. Reading is a good downtime activity.

Where are you originally from?
I am originally from Bozeman, Montana, although I was born in Mainz, Germany and did not move to Bozeman until I was three.

Where do you currently reside?
New York City.

WHAT IS A Hollywood Liberal?

TALES FROM the DUCK SIDE GOOFFELLAS

ARTIST AND WRITER: DUCK EDWING

{ *page layouts*

This book was designed by 32 senior graphic design students using Apple laptop computers and Adobe InDesign CS. Text in the book is set in Kozuka Gothic. *WORKING* was printed and Smythe-bound in a quantity of 2000 by Pragati Printing Inc. It uses 4/4 CMYK process color throughout. The cover is 110# imported premium card with matte lamination and glossy spot uv coating. The 176 page text block is 90# Bilt Emperor matte art paper, silk coat both sides with flood coating.

Mariah Anderson
pp 64-65, 84-85

Steve Apple
pp 82-83, 112-113

Lauren Brown
pp 40-41, 48-49

Jessica Bohn
pp 78-79, 120-121

Haley Couser
pp 34-35, 100-101

John Dalke
pp 130-131, 132-133, 134-135

Joe Erfle
pp 102-105,160-161

Skylar Fleming
pp 124-125, 170-171

Yuliya German
pp 42-43, 128-129

Sonja Gates
pp 92-93, 152-153, 158-159

Emily Greaser
pp 90-91, 116-117

Sarah Haggart
pp 44-45, 86-87, 108-109

Levi Hastings
pp 62-63, 94-97

Todd Heath
pp 26-27, 136-137, 168-169

Bryan Hintz
pp 46-47, 70-71

Janna Hveem
pp 52-53, 138-139

Dayel Johnson
pp 154-155, 156-157

Jeremy Johnson
pp 16-19, 54-55

Mike Kindsfater
pp 98-99, 126-127

Brian Koenig
pp 30-31, 66-69

Anneke Majors
pp 28-29, 144-145

Kevin Meyer
pp 74-75, 106-107, 122-123

Eleana Montoya
pp 24-25, 164-165

Katie Mooney
pp 76-77, 166-167

Kristen O'Toole
pp 56-57, 88-89

Jill Pancerz
pp 72-73, 142-143

Brooke Siebrasse
pp 32-33, 58-59, 118-119

Tyrell Thorton
pp 36-37,114-115

Samantha Towery
pp 50-51, 146-149

Ryan Wilson
pp 38-39, 110-111

Justin Wutzke
pp 60-61, 80-81, 140-141, 162-163

Doug Zwang
pp 20-23,150-151